THE FAKE JESUS

FALLEN ANGELS AMONG US

A Deliverance Counseling Center Publication
Pamela Sheppard, Founder and CEO

Copyright 2008 by Deliverance Counseling Center

All Rights Reserved.

ISBN-978-0-6152-1977-6

No part of this publication may be reproduced, stored in a retrieval system, or transmitted in any form or by any means___electronic, mechanical, photocopy, recording, or any other---except for brief quotations embodied in critical articles or printed reviews, without prior permission of the publisher.

Scripture taken from the King James Version

Published by

Deliverance Counseling Center
P.O.Box 356
East Greenbush, NY 12061

www.bewarechristian.com www.deliverancecounseling.com
beware911@yahoo.com

Other books by published by Deliverance Counseling Center

"To Curse the Root: A Christian Alternative to 12 Steps,
ISBN 1-4259-0766-0

"The Making of a Prophet: A Spiritual Indictment to the Organized Church
ISBN 1-4208-4725-2

"Faces of The Religious Demon: Freedom Through Deliverance Counseling. ISBN 978-1-84728-975-9

Foreword

I now see why the Lord waited 3 decades before assigning me to this particular "occult investigation." Our God is an awesome God. First, I was a student and a practitioner of the occult, then an ordained minister and an observer within the organized church, followed by a study on setting people free from demons through a unique counseling model called simply "deliverance counseling." These three spiritual paths within experiential learning definitely were required "courses" that took all of 34 years to complete in order to enter into this, the fourth course. I realize today that the first 3 courses were MANDATORY and not a drop of my time has been wasted. The Holy Ghost is never off track. The ole folk spoke true. "He may not come when you want Him, but He's always 'right on time!!!" There is a fifth and final course for me to take. Believe me---I haven't a clue.

Pamela Sheppard
Founder and Director
Deliverance Counseling Center (DCC)

CONTENTS

Chapter 1	What Has Been Goin on.	5
Chapter 2	Who Are the Endtime Players?	15
Chapter 3	Fallen Angels Among Us	27
Chapter 4	History Repeats Itself!	65
Chapter 5	An Angelic Conspiracy Theory	85
Chapter 6	The Plot Thickens!	97
Chapter 7	Church Can Be Dangerous!	107
Chapter 8	So What Happens Now?	157
	Bibliography	175
	APPENDIX	181

CHAPTER ONE
What Has Been Goin On?

In order to understand the nature of spiritual warfare, we need to have a general insight on "what has been goin on." there are a plethora of endtime books written by well meaning sisters and brothers that are too complicated for the average Christian. We have some very intelligent people in the remnant church---real deep, scholarly thinkers. The problem is that as they major on each individual tree, our minds are overrun with too many thoughts, too many ideas. The intent of each chapter in "the Fake Jesus" is to "un-complicate" things by centering on the big pieces of the puzzle in order to make the spiritual picture more understandable to the average Christian.

To get a picture of "what's goin on", it is important that we consider the intense significance of the fact that man was made a little lower than the angels. As are angels, we too are created beings. The highest created being was Lucifer, as there was no creature superior to him. Beneath Lucifer were the rest of the angelic creation: cherubim and seraphim, the arch angels, principalities and powers, the lower angels and demons. The bible also suggests that there were other living creatures on earth who themselves fell at the time of Lucifer's rebellion. It is believed that their disembodied spirits make up the lower class of demons. Of this, no one is sure. All we know is that no matter the class of demon, in the Name of Jesus, we can "cast them out!!!!"

So the bible tells us through David that we are created lower than the angels. Clearly, we were not given the power, the intelligence or even the beauty of Lucifer. We were not given either the might or the strength of principalities and powers. Nor were we given the speed and freedom of movement through the airways that demons possess. Consequently, our creation is a little lower than the angels because we are bound by gravity in a 3 dimensional world, limited by space and time. Yet in spite of our limitations, the Almighty's divine plan is to use a lower creation to rule all other creations.

This is the thorn in Satan's own side, the reason why he hates all humanity with a passion. One day, the elect shall rule Satan's kingdom as Jesus already does. As Paul wrote to the Ephesians, we have already been raised up together with Christ, seated in heavenly places. (Ephesians Ch.2) Those beings that were created before us marvel at the grace of God in terms of how He has manifested His love for us by the sacrifice of the Son of God. Once saved, even though we are a lower creation, we are yet associated with God in the heavens to rule forever in the government of the universe under the leadership of Jesus Christ of Nazareth. In truth, in eternity the first shall be last, and the last, or lower creation is first.

Even more outrageous to the devil is that God Himself took upon our human nature when He was conceived by the Holy Ghost, born of the virgin Mary. At the cross and at His resurrection, Jesus Christ of Nazareth defeated Satan clothed in a body of the lower creation and sits on the right hand of His Father in a body likened unto ours. The Lord's glorified body is immortal as our bodies shall be when He returns to raise us out of our graves and to change the bodies of the elect who are alive when He comes back.

So what does all of this mean? Lucifer, in his fallen condition -- now called Satan,--- is highly outraged that God would choose a lower creation to rule him. Man is the weapon by which Satan is defeated, because Jesus Christ defeated him as "the Son of Man." The fury of Satan's resentment toward God is seen throughout biblical history, for each time he attacks one of us, Satan's real goal is to attack God Himself for placing the power to defeat him into the hands of a creation that is inferior to him. Satan is literally OUTRAGED!!!!

In order to write this book, The Deliverance Counseling Center entered into the enemy's camp to spy out the land. In other words, we reviewed the teachings about what is referred to as "the Christ" or "the Christ Consciousness" on occult websites in order to be able to recognize teachings that emanate from a fallen angel that we call "the Fake Jesus". What we discovered is that not only have fallen angels developed a huge occult following over the last 3 decades or more, but their hidden influence is extremely powerful within the present day organized church, particularly the charismatic, word of faith movement.

Our goal with this book is to both warn and arm the elect of God and to undeceive those who unknowingly are worshiping the fake Jesus. The information we have gleaned from the ascended master teachings suggest to us that we are living in the last days, where some shall depart from the faith, giving heed to seducing spirits and doctrines of devils. Those who are lukewarm, shall be spit out of the Lord's mouth, for they are poor, blind and naked.

In Pastor Pam's third book, "Faces of the Religious Demon," various case studies are presented to reflect "faces" or "facets" of how the Fake Jesus operates. A year after the book's publication, actual names of these demons were uncovered, for in our times, fallen angels have made themselves known to their occult disciples and followers under the guise and title of "an ascended master."

Our first point to make is this.

THERE IS NOTHING NEW UNDER THE SUN!

Idolatry is not new. For an old testament Israelite, idolatry was the most heinous of crimes. In both the old and the new testament, the covenant relationship between God and His people has been represented as a marriage. Therefore, the worship of false gods was regarded as spiritual fornication or adultery---in other words---harlotry. The penalty for harlotry was death.

Even though the same demons of old testament times have continued to operate over the centuries, only the style of idolatry has changed in our times. In fact, today's "ascended masters" are most likely the same demons that operated throughout biblical history in both the old and new testament ages. Only their names have been changed. Old testament harlotry occurred in two forms: the worship of false gods or the worship of the true God by the use of images and statues.

All of the nations surrounding ancient Israel practiced idolatry in one form or another. For example, some worshiped mountains, springs, trees and blocks of stone in which the so called deity was believed to be "incarnate" in them. The Egyptians worshiped the sun, the Nile River, and animals they believed to be sacred: the bull, cow, cat, baboon, crocodile, the snake. Today, when the Holy Spirit reveals to tormented captives that a demon is manifesting in their lives, they often have had dreams of demons who confronted them in the form of these very same animals that were once worshiped as gods in the old testament. With this in mind, interpretation of these kinds of dreams is very easy. Other animals dreamed about are insects and rodents.

Among the Canaanites, worship was barbaric, degrading and often violent, including various demoralizing practices like child sacrifices, prostitution, sodomy and other degrading sexual acts. This is why there is often a strong sexual connection to idolatrous religion, and those who are tormented by a religious demon are often attacked in their sexuality. When the Israelites inhabited the lands where idolatry of this sort was practiced, God often mandated them to cleanse the area by destroying the idols which often included the livestock. Destruction was necessary due to the shameful character of the worship that was practiced, wherein sodomy was a prevalent practice.

The first cited case of idolatry among God's people is the account of Rachel's stealing of her father's teraphim. Teraphim were household gods that were small enough to be held in the hand or to sit on a stand in the house. (Genesis 31:19) Moreover, the whole book of Judges is an account of periodic apostasies, judgments and repentances where idolatry was often mixed in with the outward worship of Jehovah.

NOTHING HAS CHANGED ALONG THESE LINES EITHER. The occultists and the non-Christian religions of today have their relics and practices while those who profess Jesus Christ of Nazareth may be unknowingly worshiping the Fake Jesus as they lift up idolatrous practices within the organized church system. In one of our publications entitled "Faces of the Religious Demon," several issues on demonic religious practices within new age as well as within Christian cults and churches are addressed.

Likewise, the mediums of the old testament are referred to as "channels" in modern times. The term "medium" denotes the ability to operate as a conduit between the natural and the spiritual worlds: either the spirits of the dead which the bible refers to as "necromancy", or the spirits of non-corporeal entities, also known as demons. In practically every case, the spirit that is communicating is either a demon masquerading as the spirit of the deceased or as an angel sent from God. The most outstanding biblical account of mediumship occurred when shortly before his death, Saul sought the services of a medium in an attempt to raise up his former deceased prophet, Samuel. A spirit came forth who claimed to actually be "the ghost of Samuel." Was that "really" Samuel? The bible does not say. we suspect NOT---that it was a demon masquerading as Samuel.

Present day mediumship is at the core of the New Age belief system, and a routine practice among occultists. In this context, and under the name channeling, 21st century mediums are called "channels". Channels are demoniacally "gifted" to receive messages from a "teaching-spirit" of advanced wisdom known as "ascended masters." The usual process is telepathic, mind to mind. The ascended masters are fallen angels, cosmic beings or demons of the highest Satanic order.

In some instances, mediums (or the spirits working with them) can produce physical, paranormal phenomena such as materializations of spirits, the movement of objects, or levitation. This was the school of mediumship that our founder, Pam Sheppard was being trained for in the early 70's. She saw a few materializations but experienced no levitations---other than her spirit left her body when demons "spoke" through her. However, objects moved about her several times and continued to do so on rare occasions for at least 10 years or more, AFTER she was saved. Only once did she actually feel like she "caused" a lost object to "appear" and this occurred BEFORE she was saved. Every other time that an object moved, she had no conscious awareness that it was by a power that emanated from within or upon her.

Religious demons are not human, nor are they divine. They are simply fallen angels who began calling themselves ascended masters around the mid 20th century. In open communication with their occult disciples, we Christians have been sleepwalking in the spirit. Tenaciously focused on the contents of our own personal lives, the so called "ascended masters" have been secretly planting their seeds and working diligently toward the fulfillment of their sinister agenda. The ascended masters are in the service of their master, Sanat Kamura, --- Lucifer, the highest fallen angel that we all know as Satan or "the devil." While the higher ranking demonic have been setting the stage for "their final act" of the endtimes, rank and file foot soldiers in Satan's army were busy distracting all of us from the real issues.

Though these same demons were diligently working to stop the birth of Christ 2000 years ago, as they failed then, they will fail again. In spite of the fact that nothing or no one could stop the Lord's first coming, there are those who believe that various conditions must be met before the Lord returns to earth, this time not as a babe but as a Lion with a symbolic rod of iron in His hand and a flaming sword bursting through His mouth. What a day, what a day! The bible calls it "the Day of the Lord." In the first coming of the Lord, the of God played a significant role in preparing those involved for the Lord's birth with special visitations to Mary, Joseph, and the father of John the Baptist, Zechariah. The book of Revelation shows us angelic involvement prior to the second coming as well. Demons were also involved in the first coming, as they inspired Herod and his soothsayers to predict the signs of the time, and to conduct a relentless search for the baby Jesus by killing all male newborns from among the Israelites.

Prior to the Lord's second coming, the word of God suggests that both angels and demons will once again be extremely "active." We will need the grace and the wisdom of God to be able to discern God's messengers from the demons who work on Satan's behalf. These are some serious days. From a personal perspective, in 1985, Pastor Pam had a visitation in a dream from a 7 foot, ballheaded, muscle bound "Mr. Clean"looking being who declared himself to be "an angel sent from God." Without a doubt, Pam is one of the elect, chosen before the beginning of recorded time to be saved along with you and countless others. However, she was fooled for almost 20 years by this being. Pam thanks God every day that while she was deceived, she remained protected. She is also grateful to the Holy Ghost for exposing the deception in due season.

Since countless professing Christians are awaiting the Lord Jesus Christ to return, set up and rule His own kingdom of peace and justice on the earth, they could very well be fooled by Satan---"The Man of Sin," "the Son of Perdition," he that opposeth and exalteth himself," "the Wicked One whom the Lord shall consume with the spirit of His mouth," "he whose coming is after the working of Satan". As Jesus warned us, many false christs shall manifest in the flesh. In this regard, Fallen angels are diligently preparing to transform themselves into beings of light by manifesting in the flesh, counterfeiting the incarnation of Jesus Christ of Nazareth, born in Bethlehem 2007 years ago.

Jesus also compared the time of His return to "the days of Noah." What astounding thing happened in the days of Noah.? Fallen took on flesh, consummated the sex act with women and reproduced an offspring of giants. Noted in Genesis 6, these acts were such an offense to God that He brought about the flood to wipe away the contamination and to cleanse the earth. Since the floods of the days of Noah, fallen angels can no longer "take on flesh." As Peter reveals, those are chained up in hell. However, there are other fallen angels who are not yet chained. Could it be that these thieves and robbers are among those who will once again attempt to enter the sheepfold by "climbing up another way?" (John 10:1) These principalities and powers, the rulers of the darkness of this earth once made their abode in the heavenlies but they have apparently already "fallen to earth."

In a nutshell, this particular group of fallen angels specialize in false religion. One particular demon masquerades as Jesus Christ of Nazareth, the only begotten Son of God. Very often that demon comes into persons who have experienced being slain in the spirit. The demon that is received often calls itself "Jesus." These circumstances add understanding to what the real Jesus Christ stated as recorded in Matthew Chapter 7: Some shall prophecy, cast out demons, etc. in His name— and He is going to say "I never knew you." Perhaps the reason that Jesus never knew these professing Christians is because they were worshiping, giving praise, sending up prayers, making proclamations, making declarations in the name of a being who called himself "Jesus", yet this being is a fake. An impostor. A demon. This is certainly a plausible reason why the real Jesus does not know those who perform various exploits in His name. They were worshiping a counterfeit. **The Fake Jesus.**

CHAPTER TWO

Who Are the Endtime Players?

Our studies intensified in September 2007 when Pastor Pam happened to watch a video clip that featured the ministry of an up and coming evangelist by the name of Cindy Trimm. Stunned to watch hundreds of congregants simultaneously fall on top of each other--- slain in the spirit like waves across the entire building, Pastor Pam paid particular attention to the words of the evangelist at the moment the hundreds fell. The words were, **"I thank you, Father, that the spirit of the Ashtar has fallen upon the people."**

Troubled by the name "Ashtar", Pastor Pam searched the scriptures and found the name of an old testament idol called "Ashteroth." Once led to pursue additional research, she searched the web with the keyword "Ashtar." Shocked that a Christian evangelist would call on Ashtar moments before hundreds of the congregants fell slain, a Google search opened the door to a plethora of occult websites dedicated to uplifting the teachings of cosmic beings that are referred to as "ascended" masters.

Since September 2007, we have discovered that there are at least 50 ascended masters, perhaps even more. Fifteen of them rank as being the primary players--- fallen angels who first claimed to be aliens, sent to earth to prepare for the advent of a one world religion and the rule of the anti-Christ. Within "The Fake Jesus", we present information about the top 5: Ashtar, Jesus Sananda Immanuel, Mother Mary, St. Germain and most of all Maitreya. As the leader, Maitreya holds the title of "the Master of Masters." The following essential points are presented so that you will have a basic foundation for understanding the material you will read in the rest of the book:

- Extraterrestrial beings, aka aliens, are not "other life forms." They are fallen angels that Jesus Christ of Nazareth called DEMONS. The Apostle Paul called these cosmic beings "spiritual wickedness in heavenly(high) places, aka the skies that surround us.
- Most of these demons are "religious." They began their open, telepathic communications with mediums and psychics centuries ago.
- Knowing that they would not be well received by true followers of Christ, their work in and with the Christian churches has been and continues to be "undercover."
- There is a fake Jesus. He is not Jesus Christ of Nazareth, the only begotten Son of God. The fake Jesus is a demon that calls himself "The Christ."
- The fake Jesus identifies himself as the portrait that has hung in many churches for centuries: a Caucasian blue eyed man with long, light brown hair. The fake Jesus calls himself Jesus Sananda Immanuel.
- With his occult followers, the Fake Jesus boasts of having been the founder of various Christian cults.
- There is more than one high ranking demon who specializes in false religion. The high ranking demons call themselves "ascended masters." The "leader of leaders" calls himself "Maitreya."
- Each ascended master has a company of lower ranking demons, at least one demon assigned to every one of the elect.

Discussed in more detail in Chapter 6, very often demons who are under the authority or chain of command of the Fake Jesus enter persons who have experienced being slain in the spirit. We suspect that being slain in the spirit falls under the domain and authority of Ashtar. Whether there is a <u>true</u> manifestation of the speaking in tongues is still being tried to see if it be of God. However, what we have discovered is that there is a counterfeit of the biblical experience of which charismatics have labeled "a prayer language." We are examining whether or not the present day counterfeit of tongues is the actual manifestation of the power of the beast in the book of revelation, where it is written that the beast "calls down fire from heaven." In fact, word of faith, pentecostal and charismatic preachers and teachers often call their conferences "fire from heaven."

These questions and inquiries add understanding to what the real Jesus Christ stated: Some shall prophecy, cast out demons, etc. in His name and He is going to say "I never knew you." Perhaps the reason that Jesus never knew these professing Christians is because they were worshiping, giving praise, singing, sending up prayers, making proclamations, making declarations in the name of "another" Christ. A demon. This could be the reason why the real Jesus does not know those who perform various exploits in the name of yet "another Jesus." The Fake Jesus.

A drama has been unfolding in what we believe to be the final act upon the earth as the world has known it. We have called the main characters who strut upon the world stage of real life "the ENDTIME PLAYERS." Some endtime players are human while others are angels. God's and Satan's fallen angels are known as demons: principalities, powers, the rulers of the darkness of this world and spiritual wickedness in high or "heavenly" places.(Ephesians Ch. 6) In the book of Revelation, the Apostle John clearly presents the job description of God's angels in the last days. Simply put, angels who work for God are the agents of His wrath and judgment.

Of course the primary human players in the endtimes consist of God's people who are alive on earth when the true Jesus returns. Every one of us who is saved today believed on Jesus Christ through the gospel that the first apostles preached. In this regard, the gates of hell can never make a claim on a born again child of God because any prayer of the Lord's was answered by the Father. Therefore, the gates of hell have not and shall not prevail against the saved,whether churched or un-churched. However, it is important to point out that the Lord did not pray for the organized church in John 17. He could have, but He didn't. It was about to be formed. No, Jesus prayed for its first leaders, the 11 Apostles, with Paul being the spiritual replacement for Judas.

A serious cause for the confusion over who Jesus was referring to as "the church" is that for centuries, the organized religious system has made no distinction between its own bureaucracy and the eternal body of true believers in Jesus Christ of Nazareth. In fact, in many churches, it is assumed and presumed that those who regularly attend on Sundays, pay their tithes and offerings, and partake of the means of grace are members in good standing, and therefore they are considered "saved." This practice began with Catholicism and eventually carried over into the Protestant churches.

Nevertheless, the assumption that every one on the church rolls is saved is certainly without scriptural justification. Some of you might turn to a verse in Ephesians where Paul writes that the Lord is coming back for a church without spot or wrinkle. Charismatics, particularly those who preach "dominion theology," contend that as long as the organized church is a toothless ole hag in a soiled wedding dress, the Lord is not coming back for her. Dominion theology boasts of present day apostles who are expected to reform the organized church to cause her to be a presentable bride.

Be warned that these folk are seriously deceived because there is not one thing that man can do to affect God's timetable. Some of you "foolish virgins" need to put some oil in your lamps and come to terms with the reality that the Lord is NOT coming back for the organized church. He is coming back for his invisible, eternal kingdom made up of the elect. Once saved, we no longer have "spots or wrinkles or any such thing" because a bona fide Christian has been washed in the blood of the Lamb. Once Jesus Christ returns, we all shall finish out the cleansing by the resurrection of our dead bodies or the putting on of immortality by those of us who are alive at His coming. The final, miraculous act of the Lord at the end of this age shall be when we who are alive shall meet Him in the air along with the saved who preceded us in death before our time.

This is the gospel of Jesus Christ of Nazareth. There is only one event that I believe determines when the Lord shall come back. I believe He will come back when every name that was written in the Lamb's book of Life before the foundation of the earth was laid, has heard the gospel and has been led to the cross by the Holy Ghost. Jesus prayed that He would have ALL of the elect. If there is one among the elect who has not yet been born, He will wait on that person hearing the gospel and being drawn to Him by the Holy Ghost.

Another group of human endtime players are the false prophets. Today's men and women who call themselves pastors may feed the sheep with sermons, bible studies , even provide some occasional pastoral guidance. They may even do hospital visits. Even so, it is a rare thing to find a real biblical pastor today, who has on his or her heart not only the 99, but the one who may be in need or even in danger. As a matter of fact, our leader has been in the company of pastors who when they fellowship together in ministerial alliances and committees, they "chew the fat" by "dogging-out" those whom they pastor.

Recently, Pastor Pam had a dream that she was in attendance at a conference held by one of the most well known present day mega-tv evangelists, a pastor of a flock of 25,000 members. As is the custom, there was a room in the convention center set aside for prayer. A woman with a very small storefront church cried out loudly, "Oh, Lord! Our church is defiled. Oh, Lord, we must come before you and repent. To get rid of the uncleanness, we commit ourselves to disbanding our present fellowship and submit all that we are, all that we have been, all that we have obtained to you. We are willing to start over again! Just tell us what to do!"

Then this storefront pastor saw the mega pastor and with genuine empathy and concern bent over him and whispered in his ear,

"Brother, your church is defiled. You must repent. You can't clean up the mess yourself. You have to disband and start all over again." The mega pastor looked dismayed and puzzled. He didn't know where to begin. He had so much to lose. He didn't start out this way but with all that he had accumulated from the sheep, he had become a hireling.

Have you considered who is tending the sheep in the churches while they are being spiritually abused by hirelings? How many of today's pastors desire to rescue those who are perishing under the weight of sin? Most present day ministers know little to nothing of the dangers of occult subjection, of seducing spirits that teach and deceive. Religious demons continue to take advantage of the way that the word of God is preached and taught as their foundation for the enactment of spiritual abuse upon the sheep. The spirit of Jezebel armors itself as it seeks out pastors and church leaders who are amenable to deception as well as sheep who are prone to vulnerability. The religious demon sets the stage to preach the word of God into a defiled heart who will also teach a defiled word from the pulpit into spirits that have already been damaged, building a demonic fortress within the organized church. It appears to be a done deal.

THE ILLUMINATI

Other significant human players on today's endtime stage are called "the Illuminati." When things have gone wrong in your life, when you seem damned if you do and damned if you don't, when you look around to blame SOMEBODY, we have all pointed our finger at the invisible man. We accuse " THE MAN." The MAN may even has titles like Uncle Sam, or the Boys in Washington, City Hall, or even that low life, "Mr. Charlie." Well "the man" has yet another name. The Illuminati.

An accurate description of the Illuminati is difficult because it is a secret, ancestral, occult society, comprised of the filthy rich and often the highly educated. If you described the Mafia and threw in the flavor of Aryan Germany Nazis, and added the 32 degree freemasons into the equation, you would have a decent description of the Illuminati. The Illuminati's historic roots can be traced back to the Knights Templar, to the Greek and Gnostic initiatory cults, to Egypt and even to Atlantis.

We have reviewed the writings and testimonies of some former Illuminati's like John Todd and others who keep their real identity anonymous. Simply put, the influence of the Illuminati is staggering, crossing several systems: banking, the media, politics and the legal profession, education, labor, energy to name a few.. They also rival the Mafia in their criminal connections. As an endtime player, there influence in religion is a thing to keep a serious eye on.

The importance of the Illuminati as an endtime "religious" player is a sinister Catholic connection as depicted in the movie, Godfather III. The plot of the movie is rather similar to Satan's overall agenda--- to merge religion into the apostate one world church that will serve Lucifer. The informers warn that the Illuminati has infiltrated world governments, toward the end of bringing in a new leader who will usher in a Luciferean reign of joy, prosperity and rewards for the faithful.

The dangerous element to this group is that like Hitler and his evil regime, Illuminati members see themselves as a superior race who in their minds is not evil. The Mafia know who they are and we know who they are. However, the Illuminati consists of billionaire aristocrats who will hire "whoever" for "whatever" to control the masses. Strangely, they are convinced that their secret efforts to dominate and control the masses is for the greater good of humanity. Actually, they see themselves as "the good guys" who weed out the weak and the unfit as they develop among themselves a superior human being. The Illuminati will put it's support behind the BEAST.

Yet another key endtime player is a man called **Benjamin Crème.** Do not forget this name, saints! This white haired, pleasant, unassuming little man has been the messenger of a high ranking fallen angel whom I believe fits the biblical description of the anti-Christ better than any human being on earth. Since July 1977,Creme first contacted a demon known as an ascended master. Pastor Pam got into the kingdom just under the wire, ---4 months BEFORE this demon made his first appearance to Benjamin Creme.

For 3 decades, Creme (referred to as the John the Baptist of the anti-Christ,) has been traveling the globe, telling audiences that the second coming of Christ will not be in the clouds, but that the Christ has been here for 30 years, hiding out in the Himalayas. A British author, artist, and occult practitioner, Creme has progressively obtained worldwide credibility in high places around the world. Creme claims that the ascended masters are our elder brothers who have been stimulating and enlightening us since man's creation. Creme's main message is that Maitreya and the other ascended masters are already here and ready to solve our most critical problems.

The danger for God's people is that Benjamin Creme is considered the most credible source of information about endtime revelations. Creme has attempted to validate his claims about Maitreya by pointing to various miraculous events that have occurred around the world. For example, statues that weep real tears and blood. In England, holy messages have appeared when housewives cut the vegetables. The seeds are rearranged, spelling out the following message, "Allah is Great. Mohammad is his prophet." Healing waters have also appeared worldwide, as at Tiacote in Mexico, cures from cancer, AIDS, warts and boils have allegedly been manifested as miraculous healings. Then there is "the milk miracle" which occurred in the Hindu community, where the milk offered to the gods disappeared, as if the idols actually drank the milk. Creme claims that Maitreya and a group of ascended masters made the milk disappear.

Miraculous events of this kind significantly have yet another Roman Catholic flair about them, particularly the statutes weeping tears and blood. It is well known that the early church as well as believers who took part in the Protestant reformation believed that the beast in John's revelation was connected to Rome and the Vatican. In a news article dated May 13, 2008 written by Ariel David of the Associated Press is a stunning yet predictable statement made by Rev. Jose Gabriel Funes of the Vatican Observatory. The bold headline, "VATICAN:IT'S OKAY TO BELIEVE IN ALIENS" is reinforced by Rev. Funes:

> "How can we rule out that life developed elsewhere? Just as we consider earthly creatures as 'a brother,' and 'sister", why should we not talk about an 'extraterrestrial brother?'"

Rev, Funes statement is actually "ascended master" lingo. When ascended masters first communicated with their human subjects, they indicated that they were our "brothers," extraterrestrial aliens from outer space. The truth is that these beings are fallen ---cosmic demons. This small newspaper article is extremely important. For if Maitreya is the Beast of Revelation, than the Vatican has embraced and welcomed him into the Roman Catholic Church.

The Great White Brotherhood

Among the fallen angels, there are demons who masquerade as "the departed dead" who are also included within the inner circle of the ascended masters. The strange rational is that the term "ascended" similarly applies to deceased human beings whom new agers believe have excelled in spiritual wisdom through several reincarnations on earth. Among the top on the list of the deceased are "Mother Mary," Mary Magdelene and even a 20th century demon who claims to be the ascended "Mother Theresa."

Likewise the "ascended ones",--- both human and angelic--- have formed a demonic fellowship known among occultists and mystics as "the Great White Brotherhood." The Great White Brotherhood even claims Jesus the Christ, Gautama Buddha, and other World Teachers as their leaders, with Maitreya as "the Master of Masters." So within the White Brotherhood, the Lord Jesus Christ whom we, the elect worship, is portrayed as merely an ascended master who reports to Maitreya. Alleged to be a spiritual order from every culture and race that includes both western saints and eastern adepts, fallen among the so called White Brotherhood boast of having inspired human creativity and achievements in education, the arts and sciences, politics and religion--in other words, every worldly system and subsystem.

For example, the Fake Jesus Sananda claims that he inspired Michaelangelo's portrait of himself that the churches have accepted as the picture of "Jesus." Most churches today have pictures of the fake Jesus hanging in them somewhere. Unsuspecting believers correlate the picture of Jesus that they observe on church walls as the real Jesus when it is really Sananda. A very good deception. The church was groomed for hundreds of years by this one painted image.

Although it is alleged that the word "white" in the Great "White" Brotherhood refers not to race, but to the aura (halo) of the White Light that surrounds the saints and the sages, we have only found one "ascended master" of African descent. It should not be surprising that there is only one black man among them, since racism itself is certainly inspired by demons. We find it interesting that the nation of Islam aka "the Black Muslims" were correct about that picture of "the white Jesus." He is a fake. Not the devil himself but he is certainly "a demon.".

Certainly the white race is not "the devil" as the black Muslims taught for decades because the devil is NOT a man. However, the blue eyed, light and long haired, white skinned one is an impostor --- a top general among Satan's army. He is known as Jesus Sananda Immanuel---a fallen angel---who telepathically inspired artists to draw him in the image of a white man. The demons wisely knew that Christians would be more inclined to hang his picture on church walls if he was white as opposed to a man of color. Clearly, Sananda is well acquainted with all facets of racism. Sananda took advantage of the ignorance of racists and has successfully had a picture that represents himself=====a demon on its walls for centuries.

Most significantly, the Great White Brotherhood consistently and periodically releases its false doctrine by the spoken word through conferences, seminars, writings, books, and through personal discipleship and training, not very different from the charismatic style.

CHAPTER THREE

Fallen Angels Among Us!

In the first coming of the Lord Jesus Christ in Bethlehem, the angels of God played a significant role in preparing those involved for the Lord's birth with special visitations to Mary, Joseph, and the father of John the Baptist, Zechariah. The book of Revelation shows us that angelic involvement will increase prior to the second coming of the Lord as well. Demons were also involved in the first coming, as they inspired Herod and his soothsayers to predict the signs of the time, and to conduct a relentless search for the baby Jesus. They inspired the mass murder of all male newborns from among the Israelites.

Prior to the Lord's second coming, the word of God predicts that once again, both angels and demons will once again be extremely "active." We will need the grace and the wisdom of God to be able to discern God's angels from the demons who work on Satan's behalf. These are some serious days. Since countless professing Christians are awaiting the Lord Jesus Christ to come again, set up and rule His own kingdom of peace and justice on the earth, they could very well be fooled by Satan---"The Man of Sin," "the Son of Perdition," he that opposeth and exalteth himself," "the Wicked One whom the Lord shall consume with the spirit of His mouth," "he whose coming is after the working of Satan". Fallen angels are already prepared to transform themselves into beings of light by manifesting in the flesh, counterfeiting the incarnation of Jesus Christ of Nazareth, born in Bethlehem 2008 years ago.

As Jesus warned us in Matthew, many false christs shall manifest in the flesh. Jesus also compared the time of His return to "the days of Noah." What astounding thing happened in the days of Noah.? Fallen angels took on flesh, consummated the sex act with women and reproduced an offspring of giants. Our understanding of

Genesis 6 is that this feat was such an offense to God that He brought about the flood to wipe away the contamination and to cleanse the earth. Since the floods of the days of Noah, fallen angels can no longer "take on flesh." As Peter reveals, those are chained up in hell. However, there are other fallen angels who are not yet chained. These thieves and robbers are among those who will once again attempt to enter the sheepfold by "climbing up another way." (John 10:1) These principalities and powers, the rulers of the darkness of this earth once aboded in the heavenlies but they have apparently "fallen to earth."

Could it be that the false Christs are more angelic than they are human? Well, our strategy of research into the ascended masters' teachings is to look to the messages they impart about themselves through and to their faithful channels and followers, in other words, their human "inner circle." Clearly, our research has accounted for the fact that all demons lie. Yet we find that the ascended masters' primary weakness is pride. In their love for boasting, they not only lie, but they exaggerate and sometimes, they let the truth slip out.

ASHTAR

Along these lines, we learned that the Fake Jesus—Jesus Sananda Immanuel--- has a military general, called Ashtar. As indicated, the first time we heard Ashtar's name was in a proclamation made by evangelist Cindy Trimm as she was ministering in the slain in the spirit phenomena "in a rather astounding way" on a par, perhaps even rivaling evangelist Benny Hinn. We discovered that Ashtar serves on behalf of what these demons refer to as the Galactic Christ, Sananda.

An ascended master himself, Ashtar made his first appearance to a human being in the early 50's on July 18, 1952. As in the science fiction movie of 1951 called "the Day the Earth Stood Still," Ashtar sent messages to his real life channel, Col. George Van Tassel, to warn this country about the misuse of atomic energy. A warrior demon, Ashtar boasts that he has surrounded the earth with a legion of light numbering in the millions of allegedly benefic "guardians" who are supposed to be "looking out for" the earth and its inhabitants. In truth, these beings are just too jealous of humans to mean us any good. They lust after the very bodies that we have. However, they have proven that they DO prosper those who help them promote their blasphemous, idolatrous agenda.

Another promise Ashtar makes to his occult followers is that he and his command are prepared to evacuate and relocate our entire earth's population, if necessary, should our planet's viability be jeopardized by a geophysical or astrophysical catastrophe. Now you and I both know that this is nonsense. Earth has had some huge catastrophes already and no one has been evacuated YET! I'm sure that the inhabitants of Noah and Sodom and Gommorah would have been glad to see Ashtar!!! Even so, there are religious cults who believe this false promise, with cult leader, the late David Koresh and his Christian cult followers as the most well known example in our times.

At the very present moment, Ashtar is receiving worldwide support from international celebrity and talk show hostess Oprah Winfrey as she supports and even teaches from the occult book called "A New Earth." The following quotation from this very dangerous book made available online is a clear indication that Ashtar and the others have a plan laid out promoting a "counterfeit rapture."

> The Ashtar Command has its Headquarters on one of the large 'City' mother-ships, the "Shan Chea". This Mother Ship is over 26 miles/42km long, 8 miles/13km wide and 5 miles/8km high, with 12 major deck areas, with further Mezzanines each of 40ft/12m height. One of the middle deck areas is high enough to have its own artificial "sky" and miniature "Sun", with

green countryside, lakes and gardens below for relaxation and recreational use. The Mothership is too large to approach us closely, as its great size could adversely affect the magnetic balance of Earth's orbit. This Ship, like the hundreds of other large Mother Ships within the Ashtar Fleet, therefore has many smaller shuttle or "Scout Craft" on board which are able to approach us more closely. These are regularly used to monitor our surface and atmospheric conditions, correct geological imbalances such as potential earthquakes, or else be used to evacuate us during the major physical Earth changes.

They are able to make themselves fully visible to our physical eyesight when needed through temporarily lowering their own vibration rates down to our Third-Dimensional level. Up to now, they have not been permitted to reveal themselves until the time is correct for Earth Humans' final Ascension. Thus, when the major Earth Changes do arrive, we shall then see a great Armada of millions of Scout Ships descending from the sky to evacuate us. We will be evacuated either to the safety of the Mother Ships overhead, or else taken to the "Inner Earth" Argathian Civilization where alternative habitations have been prepared for the duration of Earth's surface cleansing.

Commander ASHTAR gives this 'overview' of the Ashtar Command and its work:

"There are millions of craft operating in this

Solar System at all times and many, many of these belong to the Ashtar Command. Some are stationed far above your Planet and are more or less stationary for long periods of time, keeping track of the Earth on their monitoring systems. Others move about, discharging their various duties. We have small scout craft doing surveying activities and we have larger craft with extended range that are capable of operating in space and which visit planets in other solar systems.

"We also have what you know as 'Mother Ships' or 'mother craft', with many smaller craft coming and going from the Mother Ship. There is thus a great deal of activity in what Earthlings think of as empty space.

"Our purpose is service, and we go where we are needed anywhere in this Sector of the Galaxy. Our Headquarters is on one of the largest of the Mother Craft, and orders and instructions come from this Craft. It is a city in itself. Most of our people are natives of one or another of the Planets within this Solar System, but also we do have those working with us from other solar systems. Our workers do visit their home Planets at various times on what you might call vacations. Most of us have worked together for a very long time; we are a well-knit Confederation and feel that we are an effective one."

[Commander ASHTAR, channeled by Gladys Rodehaver and quoted in "Ashtar: A Tribute" -

compiled by Tuella, Guardian Action Publications. The full text of "ASHTAR - A Tribute" can be read or downloaded from the link at the end of Book II]

We also have to be aware, however, that not all 'Space Ships' making contact with Earth come as representatives of the Galactic Federation of Light. Commander KORTON of the Ashtar Command, explains:

"There are those who do come, who are not from this Allegiance and who have no part in it. They come as observers and for their own ends. They are often highly scientific geniuses, and their material to their contacts can be highly impressive - indeed, almost always is. But they have come for the purpose of collecting data for their personal ends and not to give of themselves for the good of the Planet. These are not necessarily what you would call the "Dark Forces", which is yet of another deeper allegiance.

"Now the so-called "Dark Forces" (a balancing agent in the Cosmos) are those of our own Galaxy who are still openly opposed to the Brotherhood of Light, its principles and standards and goals for mankind and the Planet Earth. They would seize the Planet if that were possible, to control it for their own purposes, which would destroy the freedom of Man. Commander Ashtar has been one of the most staunch defenders of the freedom of Man and his inherent right to choose, to decide to

> fashion his own embodiment, without outside pressures put upon him.
> "The bands of renegades that patrol the terrestrial realms are immediately dispatched to their proper level when overtaken in trespassing activities within this Solar System. The Fleets of the Heavenly Commands are prompt to transport such intruders in masterly fashion."

The sheer magnitude surrounding the fact that Oprah Winfrey is a teacher and disciple of this book does not require any further comment. However, it should be noted that the Mother Ship teaching is not new---a sign that Ashtar's influence was felt two decades before his encounter with Col. Van Tassel. It was also taught in the 30's under the leadership of Elijah Muhammad and continued in the 60's by Malcomb X. As the African American counterpart to the muslim faith---founded in the 1930's, the Nation of Islam is a religious organization whose present day leader is Minister Louis Farakkan. The Muslim Mother Ship studies are extremely "similar" to that found in "the New Earth," only the Mother Ships of Islam were only rescuing Black Muslims.

The Nation of Islam is a religion formed as a result of its founder's visionary and face to face contact with a cosmic being who called himself "Master Fard Muhammad." As a channel for a "master," it should be noted that the founder of the NATION OF ISLAM was also a son of a Baptist preacher. His name was changed from Elijah Poole to the Honorable Elijah Muhammad. Here is a summary quotation of Elijah Muhammad's teachings on the Mother Ship:

> "The mother ship is one-half mile by one-half mile in size. It remains primarily in outer space but enters the Earth's atmosphere every six months "to take on air." He taught that the purpose of the Mother Ship was to "destroy the

white man's world." In Nation of Islam esoteric symbolism, white, black, red and yellow "people" were symbols of states of mind. Very few people in the Nation, however, are aware that most of the doctrine was given metaphorically and symbolically. The rank-and -file membership considers the teachings to be "actual facts."

According to Elijah Muhammad, Ezekiel's vision of wheels is said to be a vision of the Mothership. 4500 bombs would all strike land. None will fall into water. America is to be the first nation the Mothership will attack. Before striking and releasing its bombs, it will drop leaflets printed in English and Arabic warning of the coming destruction. Some unspecified time later it would emit a high-pitched, piercing sound to warn that the attack is imminent. At that point, it will be too late. The destruction will commence.

Elijah Muhammad once gave a strong clue that the Mothership teaching was also symbolic. He wrote that Master Fard Muhammad told him that the ship flew 40 miles above the Earth's atmosphere but that he thought that the 40 miles was a sign of his own 40 year mission. Elijah Muhammad taught that there were two safe places to which people could flee to and reside to survive the destruction brought on by the Mothership. After the bombing, America would burn for 310 years and require 690 years to cool off. After the destruction, a "new world" would be born and "a new God" would bring in "a new Islam" and "a new Quran."

As you read, certainly you noted some of the similarities and variations on the Mother Ship theme between the "the New Earth" excerpt and the summary outline from Elijah Muhammad's teachings. It should also be evident that the ascended "masters" have been channeling their own religions on this earth for quite some time. Even the Mormons have a "Mother Ship" teaching. The danger the world is facing as a result of the book "the New Earth" is beyond our ability to estimate, for when Oprah endorses a book, it becomes a best seller overnight. We cannot compete with Oprah's influence. We are like Gideon, with only a few to help. We can also relate to David with a handful of stones against a Goliath like Oprah. And like the boy with the fish sandwich, only God Himself can multiply and feed the people, compared to the countless millions that Oprah reaches daily through every avenue of mass communication. Oprah claims to be a Christian and therefore she is no different from   several other mainline Christian leaders who offer seminars that focus on territorial principalities and powers.

According to the word of God, believers have the authority to cast out demons from humans in the name of our Lord. However, even though we may find ourselves wrestling with these beings to set ourselves or someone else free, we have no power to "pull fallen angels out of their place in the heavenlies." If we think we do, then we are walking on some very dangerous ground.   What the brethren need to know is that Satan WILL have his day. Though his day will be short, we will not be able to stop him because God Himself has given Satan the opportunity to prove whether or not he can bring peace to the world and also be worshiped "as god" by the world and the apostate church. Then the real Jesus comes out of the clouds and shows both the wicked trinity of the the two beasts and the dragon "whose the Boss!!!"

Ashtar and the other cosmic demons are very zealous to maintain a stance of brotherhood and they avoid like the plague to be perceived as evil. Their rebellion is "different"from rank and file demons. These "higher level" beings desire to be pleasing to man. Nevertheless, their sin is even worst than the evil, low level demons who actually acknowledge that Jesus Christ of Nazareth is Lord. As a biblical example, consider the python demons of divination that Paul cast out from the female psychic. These demons recognized both the Lord and His disciples. (Acts16:16-18)

Actually, the sin of the ascended masters is worst then that of lower level demons because the ascended masters deny our Lord's divinity as the ONLY begotten Son of God, claiming that they themselves are the Christ. Their blasphemy will earn them the hottest jail cells in the lake of fire. Consequently and in the meantime, it is imperative that the ascended masters maintain an "air of peace." However, apparently some of their own occultist channels and followers were attacked by demons who claim they too are a part of Ashtar's Command. It bares repeating that Satan's kingdom is divided on the astral level.

So through telepathic communication with a channel, Ashtar sent out a defensive word of caution to his followers, and for all the gobbledygook, here is a paraphrase of Ashtar's claim:

> "Look you guys. If any of you have been tormented, it was not from us. There is a fake Ashtar Command that is imitating us. Renegade demon cadets who were trained in the Ashtar command who did not measure up were expelled. Resentful and envious, they formed their own battalion, a duplicate of us but operated by demons who are assigned to the lower planes closest to Earth . These renegades have formed alliances with other rebellious demons who have sided against me. This rebellious group tells its channels that it is me, --Ashtar-- and they even imitate Sananda."

Think of it!!! According to Ashtar, the so called impostor demons of the Ashtar Command are very dangerous. They are fear based. They threaten, chastise, promote paranoia, prophesy fearful scenarios of Earth' devastation---real horrific, terrifying stuff. They also incite racial and religious discrimination. They will pressure those they are able to "channel with" to commit suicide, take drugs, become irresponsible by deserting their families, dropout of society or live an unbalanced life. They also encourage people to give over their money to charlatans and deceivers. They cause their captives to give their personal and spiritual authority to another. They also cause mental illness.

In truth, when we reviewed Ashtar's warning to "his people," we were astounded. His warning is quite eerie because Ashtar has provided a classic profile of those cases that have come before us either for deliverance counseling, or people who consistently email or contact us for advice or prayer. In "Faces of the Religious Demon," Pastor Pam presents several cases that perfectly fit every facet of Ashtar's description of demonic torment. Although these demons may or may not have rebelled against Ashtar, we suspect that the renegade demons are also under the command of the Fake Jesus.

This warning came from such a high level cosmic demon,--- Ashtar--- the right hand warrior of the Fake Jesus, addressed to occult, new age practitioners, mediums and channels about some renegade demons who are imitating his squad, no less. Deep stuff!!! So when we "tried the spirits on this, we asked ourselves 2 questions: "Is Ashtar telling the truth or has he and his troops been attacking their own followers?" Even though all demons are liars, we tend to believe the former. From our studies, high level cosmic demons do not appear to torment those whom they have recruited.

In making such a supposition, we consider their goals and their mission. For example, the Ascended Masters are charged with "winning the world" for their master Sanat Kamura through humanitarian acts. Therefore, they try to distance themselves from open acts of darkness. In fact, high level channels and ascended master disciples like Benjamin Crème and others that are presented in upcoming chapters as well as their present day counterparts have all prospered, had longevity and were not tormented throughout their lives. In death, Most assuredly they open their eyes in the tormenting flames of hell, but like the rich man in the Lord's parable,"they had it good while they lived." (Luke 16)

Actually, the ascended demons encourage humans to find their own divinity. They preach what you have heard from Kenneth Copeland and many other prominent Christian ministers ---that we are gods with a little "g." Astoundingly, both the occult and the Christian followers and disciples of the god-man teaching are in the millions, perhaps billions. Likewise, the ascended masters consistently declare "let your own soul be your guru, for you too are divine!" In addition, these fallen, cosmic demons show no interest in the personal life of human beings. Our founder can relate. When Pastor Pam was recruited to be a channel for an ascended master back in the 70's, the higher level demons showed absolutely no interest in her questions about her career or her love life as did the lower level demons. In her own words:

> "Lower level demons were involved in my life with every dumb detail like, "the food you ate last night was too salty, Dearie!" Not so with the higher ranking demons. As I was bored with religion, they looked down on my carnal concerns. Cosmic demons will offer advice but they tend not to set themselves up to control every aspect of their channels' lives as do demons who monitor our every move.

Ascended demons are also known to lift up, honor and respect man's free will. Their byword is 'we are already divine. We are here to encourage you in your own spiritual walk toward godhood, for you are divine also!!!' Reminds me of Al Pacino's movie 'the Devil's Advocate.' These demons work on man's primary weaknesses: ego, vanity and pride. Some deep stuff. The more mature we become in our Christian walk, the more the sophisticated demons are assigned to us."So our goal with this book is to issue a clear warning.

Ashtar is an angelic military general of generals. Simply put, there are no warring demons who do not come under Ashtar's command, either directly or indirectly. Even though Ashtar's works and his workers are invisible, their influence can be detected by two primary activities: the empowerment of false prophets and the release of a false "feeling" through altered states of consciousness.

A false prophet is of two varieties: one is a somewhat innocent bystander seduced by deception and delusion while another is an evil perpetrator planted among Christians by deliberate design. From what we have seen, most of these so called men and women of the cloth have been deceived primarily because they did not try the spirits to see if they be of God. The thin line between the deceived and the deliberately false is of no consequence because the results are the same. In short, the damage to the sheep is staggering, pervasive and far-reaching.

For example, consider Todd Bentley and the Lakeland Florida outpouring of supernatural manifestations. Since April 2008, called a world wide revival, Bentley began his meeting with a seating capacity of 1200, to a 3000 seat capacity, to an 8000 seat facility and to a 15,000 seat stadium in a month's time. With much excitement amid controversy, the Internet contains a plethora of articles on both sides of the question as to whether or not Todd Bentley is a false prophet. Between his body covered in tattoos and his unorthodox healing practices that include kicking sick people in the gut to generate a healing and such other questionable behavior, people are examining each tree and not looking at the surrounding forest.

The bottomline is that Todd Bentley has been deceived,---duped actually---by demonic visitations of fallen angels who work under the authority of Ashtar's command. Regardless of the names that these beings have called themselves, they are branded with Ashtar's calling card. Clearly, Todd Bentley is sincere and not a deliberate false prophet by design primarily because the information that we have used to try the spirits came out of Bentley's own mouth from bits and peices of his personal testimony. First of all, Bentley's first encounter is quite similar to the testimonies of reported alien abductions, an Ashtar command trademark. Bentley states that "he was beamed up through a pillar of fire portal to an operating table in heaven with two angels on either side of the table." Bentley also acknowledges that he was sawed in half, that his guts popped out and that he was "stuffed with boxes." Doesn't sound like the work of an angel sent from God.

In yet another statement, Bentley reports that he first saw an angel called "Healing Revival" on December 5, 2000. In Bentley's own words, Bentley states "God also revealed to me that this angel was involved in the ministry of John Lake, William Branham and John Knox in Scotland." Bentley claims that God told him that "this angel is from the North West Healing Revival and is manifesting again as a sign that God is restoring the Voice of Healing Revival and opening up the ancient wells. In our ministry, over the last year, this angel has come frequently and on many different occasions. When he comes, I get a gift---the ability to diagnose people's sicknesses with my left hand. And whenever this angel shows up, the miracles go off the charts. Instead of a few healings, we'll get three blind eyes in one night or maybe a cripple guy gets out of a wheelchair." (www.etpv.org/2003/angho.html)

Another excerpt from Bentley's testimony reveals the secret, underhanded mission of Ashtar: In Bentley's own words in a youtube video clip, "Lord, why can't I just move and forget about all that other stuff." His response allegedly from God laid out Ashtar's goal: "The people already believe in Jesus BUT THE CHURCH DOESN'T BELIEVE IN THE SUPERNATURAL. TODD, YOU'VE GOT TO GET THE PEOPLE TO BELIEVE IN THE ANGEL!" Ashtar's sentiments exactly----to release an ability among millions of people to make contact with angels through visions and other supernatural means. As Bentley pointed out in a televised interview, "the purpose of the Lakeland Florida experience is to get the attention of the world through its fascination with the supernatural. Just as with an illusion a semblance of the truth can be found, likewise supernatural phenomena sent by fallen angels can resemble divine manifestations when these beings transform themselves into angels of light. The fake Jesus is astute at producing revelations, prophecies and even miracles and healings.

For a future article or book, we will study this subject to ascertain how these supernatural phenomena are brought about among professing Christians. In the meanwhile, we speculate that demons have found a way to manipulate the subliminal portion of our flesh in order to imitate what is commonly referred to by Christians as "the anointing"--- where the heart of man becomes an open doorway or portal. Todd Bentley is quick to point out that his Florida meetings are characterized by the ability of the congregants to feel what they believe to be the tangible presence of God. It seems that the Ashtar command works within this realm of false mysticism. Those under the power of the human sub-conscious are subject to a difficult to describe manifestation, often compared to an electric current passing through the body. The more that we surrender to this "feeling" we call "the anointing," the more power we give to fallen angels to control us. The Ashtar Command is preparing millions of people to "believe in the angel," perhaps in preparation to believe on the two beasts of the book of Revelation known as the the false prophet and the anti-christ. We suspect that these two beasts are the same fallen angels who are known as Sananda and Maitreya.

SANANDA

Sananda's "prophetic leanings" are a strong indication that he may be the second beast in the book of Revelation, known as the false prophet. As an example, here is a prophecy that Sananda channeled through his first prophetess, known as Thedra:

> So be it I have appointed thee Mine spokesman; I've given unto thee the power and authority to speak for being that which I AM. And I say unto thee Mine child whom I have called forth and anointed thee with the Holy Spirit, thy name shall be as it is now called, Thedra - that name I spoke unto thee from out the ethers, and thou heard Me and accepted that which I gave unto thee; and wherein have I deceived thee? Wherein have I forgotten thee, or left thee alone?'
>
>> 'I say unto thee, Mine hand is upon thee and I shall sustain thee and you shall come to know that which I have kept for thee. So be it that I have kept thy reward and at no time shall it be dissipated or scattered, for it is intact. So let this Mine Word suffice them which question thee - let them question, and I shall bear witness for thee. For do I not know Mine servants from the traitor? Do I not reward Mine servants according unto their works or merits? I speak that they might know that I am mindful of Mine servants, that I am not a poor puny priest who has forgotten his servants.'
>
> 'I say unto them, Mine servants shall be glorified above the crowned heads of the nations which have

> set themselves apart, and denied Me Mine part of Mine word - for they have turned from Me in their conceit and forgetfulness.'
>
> 'Now let this go on record as Mine Word, and I shall give unto them proof, which are of a mind to follow Me.
>
> So be it as I have spoken and I am not finished; I shall speak again and again, and I shall rise Mine Voice against them which set foot against Mine servants, and they shall be as ones cast out. So let them ask of Me and I shall enlighten them. So be it I know where of I speak. Be ye as ones blest to accept Me and know Me for that which I AM.

For those of you who are familiar with word of faith and pentecostal prophecies that are routinely uttered in their worship services and meetings, you will note a very similar phraseology and tone to this utterance. In fact, if someone stood up in your church and uttered these very same words, practically no one would suspect that this particular prophetic utterance emanated from Sananda. With this "word,", a fallen, cosmic demon gave "his prophetess", Sister Thedra, the authority to use the name "Sananda." The remainder of this "prophecy" is as follows:

> 'Now it is come when ones which have the will to follow Me shall come to know Me by that name which I commanded thee to give unto the world as Mine 'New name.' There are many that shall call upon the name of Jesus, yet they will deny the new name as they are want to do. While unto thee I give assurance that I am the One sent that there be Light in the world of men. Now let

this be understood, that they that deny Mine New Name deny Me by any name.

'Sori Sori: Mine hand I have placed upon thine head, and I have given unto thee the authority to use Mine name. Give unto them the name Sananda, by which they shall know Me as the Lord thy God - the Son of God sent that ye be made to know Me, the One sent from out the inner temple that there be Light in the world of men.'

Born in 1900 in Mount Shasta California and formerly known as Dorothy Martin, Dorothy was renamed "Sister Thedra." A well respected new age channeler of the 20th century, Thedra was appointed by the referenced prophecy as Sananda's prophetess, just as Benjamin Creme is the prophet for Maitreya. Thedra herself was duped and remained deceived until her death. While in her 50's in 1954, Thedra became terminally ill with cancer when a being who called himself "Jesus" suddenly materialized at her deathbed and instantly healed her by the laying on of hands. He then sent her forth with "Go, feed my sheep and I will give you the food."

Deathbed visitations are common with Sananda. In particular, those out of body death experiences that have become so well known in our generation are orchestrated by Sananda and the religious demons under his command. We in no way marvel at Thedra's alleged healing. Since Sananda or one of his demons who specializes in inflicting sickness and disease put the cancer on Dorothy Martin in the first place, a simple withdrawal of his hand from the sickness cleverly caused Thedra to assume that Sananda healed her when all he did was stop "making her sick!". No wonder Thedra was a faithful follower of Sananda until she died at the ripe ole age of 92. What a shock it must have been for Thedra to realize that she had been duped by a master magician, the fake Jesus himself when she opened up her eyes in hell.

With the word above, Sananda "anointed" Thedra and drew her into full scale blasphemy. He gave Thedra the authority to use what he referred to as "his rightful name." As the fake Jesus, this impostor demon pointedly emphasized that he was of the Kumara line. One of Satan's names among newagers is Sanat Kumara. Therefore, referring to himself as Sananda Kumara is simply another way of saying that he is in the family of Satan. As to his main channel, Thedra worked hard for Sananda. In 1961, she founded the Association of Sananda and Sanat Kumara. At that time, Thedra received a series of lessons from Sananda, as well as founded a newsletter to advise and assist their followers through what occultists call "Earth's coming transformation." Ironically, we have a similar purpose for our newsletter called, "Try the Spirits"----to advise and assist the elect NOT to be deceived prior to "the earth's coming transformation", the return of the true Jesus, King of Kings and Lord of Lords, Jesus Christ of Nazareth!!!

It seems that the year 1900 as well as the decade of the 1950's were significant for fallen angels to stabilize their last work. As previously menthoned, the Sananda influence even permeated Hollywood by the release of a science fiction movie in 1951 entitled "The Day the Earth Stood Still." Inspired by a short story authored by a science fiction writer by the name of Harry Bates, this movie cleverly embraced the Maitreya-Sananda message, namely that the cosmic beings that surround the earth are benefic and wise, with better character than any of earth's human sinners.

In the movie, an alien lands on this planet and warns the rebellious people of Earth that they must live peacefully or be destroyed. A robot and what we call "a demon posing as a man from outer space" held the world spellbound with startling and miraculous powers. Sounds like the anti-christ, doesn't it?!!! Since ascended masters claim to inspire the arts, we suspect that Sananda telepathically inspired this very provocative movie of the early 50's to subliminally prepare the hearts of men for what lies ahead.

While Sananda was inspiring Hollywood and simultaneously recruiting Thedra, yet another channel "was anointed" in the 50's--- George King--- a male counterpart to Thedra, also born in 1900. George King, an avid yoga practitioner and British occultist for 10 years at the time of his visitation, was sent a messenger, a demon called Aetherius. Through the assistance of this demon, the Aetherius Society was begun in London in 1954. King was told to prepare himself to become the voice of the Interplanetary Parliment, so in 1955, King was named as the "primary terrestrial mental channel."

Until his death in 1982, King regularly channeled messages from Aetherius as well as Sananda. It is very significant to note that George King was consecrated as an archbishop of the Independent Liberal Catholic Church. The Liberal Catholic Church is one of thirty or more Catholic Churches in the world which are independent of Rome, such as the Greek Orthodox, Coptic, Old Catholic, etc. The strange beliefs of various catholic sects are so bizarre that it would take too many issues to present them. Suffice it to say that just as you will find perhaps billions of innocent people who are extremely devoted to Allah, Buddha, and other gods-- sincere people, faithful followers of the wrong god,--- Sananda and other fallen angels have used the same tactics within organized churches that call themselves "Christian."

The strategy to obtain channels and other followers is relatively routine among the masquerading demons. First of all, religious demons never tell their human targets the dirty, down and dark side of their real mission and purpose. Nor do they reveal that they actually serve Satan. Yet, not denying their god, they just switched a few letters around and refer to Satan as "Sanat" Kamura. These so called "ascended masters" lure and entice people to follow them either directly or indirectly-----authoring books through them and prospering their lives in material and carnal ways. Channels are attracted to and lured by the positive side of the message based upon the desires of their own hearts. And since the human heart is deceitfully or secretively wicked, these human channels have not been difficult targets for deception by high level fallen angels whose commander in chief is Satan.

Clearly, with professing Christians who serve and worship the true Jesus Christ of Nazareth, the only begotten Son of God, Sananda and his demon and human helpers must resort to deception. Their strategy is to employ counterfeit manifestations of the spirit so as to infiltrate the minds of professing Christians to accept false practices, false doctrine and the deceptions of false prophets. Even though Sananda is the chief demon that imitate the Son of God, other demons play a part in what they refer to as "the Christ consciousness." Imitation of Jesus Christ of Nazareth by Sananda and the others is either with or without the cross or without the resurrection or at times, even without BOTH.

For example, through several channels, Sananda basically reports that at the cross, he was not dead but comatose and that the other Ascended Masters revived him and he fled to India. No surprise. The Fake Jesus defies the resurrection. The demon Sananda was certainly at the cross invisibly, yet not on the cross physically, As Sananda mocked the true Jesus with the rest of the demons---the ones whom King David prophesied as "the bulls of Bashan," (Psalm 22) but at the cross, Sananda was merely a disembodied demon among the crowd of humans and demons. The results of our study have shed light on why so many churchgoers have not understood the bodily resurrection of the Only Begotten Son of God. They have been unknowingly worshiping the fake Jesus, Sananda Immanuel---the one who denies the Lord's bodily resurrection.

As one manifestation of the Fake Jesus, Sananda's influence is more apparent among the Mormons, Roman and Independent Catholics, the Christian Scientists, the 7th Day Adventists, the Jehovah Witnesses, and other so called Christians that have changed the word of God, some of them "ever so slightly."

Each of these allegedly Christian sects have perverted the gospel in one way or another. However, this "impostor god" has also drawn out followers through the preaching of the prosperity message, "a millionaire Jesus." "Name it and claim it" is also a Sananda influence. We are gods with a small "g" is straight up Sananda. Kingdom theology. Peace and unity. Let's take the kingdom and put our foot on the devil. In other words, word of faith, non-denominational, charismatic and Pentecostals have more imperceptibly changed the nature and character of Jesus Christ of Nazareth with their "new doctrines" and their neglecting to preach the true meaning of the cross and the Lord's bodily resurrection.

Consequently, it could very well be that there are very few bona fide Christians who have not come under Sananda's influence, more or less. Those who came to know Jesus Christ through the organized church have come to know the Jesus of their understanding, embraced him, fallen in love with his compassion, his suffering, his goodness, his mercy, his peace, his power to heal. Countless of them became devoted followers of the Jesus of their understanding. However, without an understanding of the Lord's bodily resurrection and the true meaning of the cross, neither the devoted believer nor the hypocrite is saved. The expression "He rose from the dead" has become meaningless, religious verbiage,--a lifeless "tag on" to the cross. In spite of the fact that the devoted followers are initially deceived by the attack they have received from the hands of Christian hypocrites, the Lord Jesus Christ of Nazareth uses the attack to His own advantage by calling out those that He has chosen from the beginning of time to be genuinely saved.

Here are a few recent examples of some seminars and training programs with a subtle Sananda influence. Those who sent out these announcements are "up and coming mega wannabees," pretty well known even without national television exposure.

Example #1 This is a telephone conference, offering degrees from the associates to the doctoral level in intercessory prayer. Think of it. You can become Dr. So and So, a Phd by in prayer. The title of these teachings is called: Manning the Witching Hour. Take a look at the course subjects:

Territorial Warfare Prayer--Gap Warfare--- Warfare on the Wall---I Intercession through Praise & Worship, Listening Prayer--- Targeting Warfare Prayer---Strategic Intercession---Prophetic Intercession---- Apostolic Authority in Prayer---Foundational Prayer Principles---Dealing with High Places in Intercession---- Participating Students may receive Associate thru Doctorate Degrees in Intercessory Prayer
. *Tuition Cost: $150.00 per month*

Example #2 This is yet another out of context teaching which is intended to appear to be based on new and fresh revelation, taken out of the old testament. We don't have to explain. Read it for yourself.

We are presently living in the Hebraic Year 5868 and the Roman year 2008. The number "8" is depicted by the letter chet. This character pictures a wall, a fence. This is the year to open the gates. In times of great transition, one must be willing to allow the Lord to redirect your steps. If He asks you to let go of one thing to embrace another, then you can believe the Lord will open the new gate He directs you to pass through! Although we had planned to begin our 2008 Conference schedule in Atlanta , the Lord has redirected our steps and instead led us to begin in Ohio. So we want to invite each of you to join us in Middletown, Ohio for Opening the Gates of Revelation: A Time to Prophesy to All Dry Bones!

The first of these gatherings will be in Middletown, Ohio as we open up the gates of revelation - personally, corporately, territorially and generationally. The dates of this conference actually fall within the Hebraic month of Nissan, which is biblically understood to be a time to decree (by speech) your future. So whether your home, family, workplace, church, city or nation is contending to pass through a new gate of opportunity, this will be a time when your faith will be stirred so that your mouth aligns with and declares the purposes of Heaven. Prophetic Prophetic ministry teams will be available, so each registrant will also have an opportunity to receive personal ministry.

The first thing you should notice about both seminars is that they are much too complicated. The Hebraic year? So what? The truth is that every prophetic seminar has "a hook" that appeals to the intellect. You will notice that each prophet will copy the other by giving every new year a unique title. Many of them in 2008 have a phrase that the prophets are labeling "opening the gates of blessing." Most of them are selling themselves as present day Isaacs, who have the power to speak special blessings into your lives. Such a thing borders on witchcraft. Isaac was not even a prophet. The other old testament prophets did not imitate Isaac as each one of them was unique. Yet today, every person who is calling themselves a prophet is claiming to have the power to change your life with their so called "anointed" words of knowledge. We must all be careful.

Within this framework, we should also remember the Lord's warning to His disciples about what the last days shall be like for the elect. Brother shall give up brother and literally become spies for the anti-Christ once he is revealed and "descends" from the air to assume power on earth. For this reason and several others, we consider it wise to remain both harmless yet wise. As we warn others, we fear no one. We choose to remain "a voice, crying in the wilderness" through counseling, mentoring and our books as we serve those who have "an ear to hear." As such, we are not trying to start any movements or attract any disciples. Several well meaning ministers have offered to connect us to their various Christian networks. We have been respectful and simply not taken them up on their generous offers. In reverse, we do not routinely offer ourselves to teach anyone unless we are invited by them to do so. We heed the warning of the Apostle James. Be not many masters for yours is the greater condemnation.

As we ourselves have been sincere but "sincerely wrong" on the very same spiritual matters that we are now warning others to avoid, so are countless others in the same situation---people who even have large crowds supporting and defending them. A little correction here and there would be of great value to many, yet there are some so called Christians who are so spiritually proud that they can't conceive even the possibility of admitting to even ONE error---especially if it is pointed out to them by someone whom they do not deem to be "noteworthy.". These are the deluded to the "nth" degree. For them, our feet don't even touch the dust as we speed by them like roadrunner. There is just too much confusion in the land. Consequently, we do not attempt to either persuade or convince those who are too proud to admit to error. It doesn't matter to us whether they are "mega" or "tiny." Error is error regardless of who the perpetrator may be.

So, here goes!!! The reason why we have some serious reservations about seminars that call themselves "spiritual warfare," "intercessory prayer," and gatherings of today's self proclaimed prophets who use terms like "opening the gates" is because those who teach such subjects are like the blind leading the blind. Even if they have the gift of discernment and can actually SEE into the spirit realm, they do not realize that their vision is merely a mirage, for fallen are like skillful magicians. They will open up the veil and let us peak, and then stand back and laugh at us when we buy into their lie, hook line and sinker. Most importantly, the Lord Jesus Christ of Nazareth never gave us a specific "spiritual warfare" or "intercessory prayer" assignment. All He commanded us to do is " cast out devils."

In other words, occupy until He returns. Even though the Lord instructs us to pray, "thy kingdom come, they will be done on earth as it is in heaven," the Lord's teaching on prayer was a subtle way of saying to His followers, "Pray for My Return." Why? Because the Lord knew that God's will would NOT be done on earth as it is in heaven, until He comes back to reign and rule earth Himself!!!! We can certainly ask for God's will to be done in our lives and the lives of people we pray for. When we know His will, then we pray it. When we don't, then we pray, "Lord, teach me your will in this situation." We pray nothing else about it until He reveals His will. If He doesn't reveal His will, then "we leave the issue alone." Prayer is simple. Example #1 concerning "territorial prayer" complicates prayer and opens the door wide to demonic deception.

Consider Daniel. When Daniel prayed, his prayers caused an angelic battle that Daniel himself was completely unaware of in the spiritual realm. When prayer is in accord with God's will, we do, in a sense, affect angelic battles. However, to take prayer to a level of actually attempting to control what goes on between angels and demons ---when we try to "bring down principalities and powers"---we believe that we are stretching our self-created teaching on spiritual warfare beyond the limits and boundaries of our actual authority. God Himself have given Satan and his army "the go ahead." Its a challenge where the Lord mocks the demons in derision with, "Hey Satan. You will have no lasting success in your attempt to rule the world--- but have a go!!! Take your best shot. I am counting on My Son and I am counting on the elect to stay loyal to Me and they will spit in the face of the anti-Christ, the False Prophet----- and you, devil!!!."

So what they do is God's business and the devil's business. We can't stop with prayer what the Lord Himself has decreed as "His will." For Satan to "have a go" is a part of the Lord's will. Satan's time is real short, a blink in God's eye. Simply put, Jesus does not need us to mess with cosmic demons. Even Michael, God's top angel did not mess with Satan over the dispute over the body of Moses and simply said, "the Lord rebuke thee." (Jude:9) Other than for Satan himself, even Sananda can't mess with Michael!!! Do we have the power, the authority and the might of Michael? No---we do not!.

We certainly have the authority to cast out demons here on earth. But the heavens? Well, THATS yet another story!! We do NOT have the authority to "MAN THE WITCHING HOUR!!!! That's the job of God's angels and they are "on the job." Simply put, the Lord has his own angelic troops to contend with Satan and his army. While on earth, Jesus was rather casual about it when he stated, "I can call on 12 legions ofangels ." He is even more powerful since His Resurrection and Ascension. Actually, the triune God has at least 2/3 more angels than Satan has demons and He can create more angels if He chooses to. Satan has all the demons he is ever going to get. In truth, we should have nothing to say to angels----PERIOD!!!!! Leave them to the Lord.

MAITREYA

Although he is called "the Christ"---the Master of Masters-- by his occult followers, thus far, Maitreya has primarily concentrated his efforts toward eastern religions and new age occultism, relegating the "Christian" emphasis into the hands of Jesus Sananda Immanuel, Ashtar, Mother Mary, St. Germain and other demons. Since both Maitreya and Sananda are the two main fallen angels who masquarade as the Lord, it seems to fall into place that Sananda and Maitreya may be the two beasts of Revelation, namely the Anti-Christ and the False Prophet.

As we have continued to examine literature on the ascended masters, the automatic writings of those who channel telepathic communications from high ranking demons claim that various ascended masters have already "manifested in the flesh." These so called embodied cosmic beings claim to be overseeing the spiritual development of the human race on both an individual level and on a global plane. According to various accounts, there is a distinct hierarchy of fallen angels in operation to build a kingdom for their master Sanat Kamura. Through consciousness-altering techniques of yoga, transcendental meditation, channeling, chanting, drugs and hypnosis, millions of New Agers have allegedly received visitations from disembodied beings who have masqueraded as benevolent spirits, duping their hosts into believing that they are sent from God to fulfill His Divine Plan. Yet. as depicted in the Book of Genesis, it is a more highly favored achievement for a fallen angel to be able to manifest in the flesh as they did in the days just prior to the flood. In the Lord's warnings about the last days just prior to His second coming, Jesus compared the endtimes to "the days of Noah."

According to Benjamin Creme, Maitreya descended in July 1977, allegedly from His ancient retreat in the Himalayas and took up residence in the Indian-Pakistani community of London. Furthermore, Creme alleges that Maitreya has been living and working there, seemingly as an ordinary man, with his true status known to relatively few. He has been emerging gradually into full public view so as "not to infringe upon humanity's free will."

Not so. Maitreya descended from higher than the Himalayas. He descended from second heaven. Creme himself has been lied to, deluded and deceived, because the agenda of "the god of this world"is to rule all humanity at any cost.Since demons are infamous liars, don't believe for one minute that Maitreya is embodied 24-7. He is a fallen angel, who like the other ascended masters that Maitreya is "the master of masters" of, they can only function as we do on earth by taking over the body of a human being who has opened the door to them by submitting their free will to consciousness altering techniques. Religious demons have more than merely infringed on free will, but have literally stolen the bodies and souls of the vulnerable.

Since July 1977, through Benjamin Creme and the undercover work of a multitude of lower ranking ascended masters and religious demons under Maitreya's command, the Masters of Masters has been diligently and secretively preparing humanity for his outward presence, particularly for the day that the bible calls "the abomination of desolation." On this horrendous day, the anti-Christ shall enter the temple and declare Himself to be God and those who serve him now, shall worship him then.

July 1977 is rather significant because Pastor Pam was born again just 3 months prior to Maitreya's appearing to Benjamin Creme. In spite of the fact that a being materialized before her eyes in 1975, Jesus Christ of Nazareth saw to it that Pastor Pam "made it in" to the kingdom of God, just under the wire. Paul warned the Corinthians that the god of this world has the power to blind the lost from being saved, and in other parts of the scripture, there is a warning of deception even for the very elect. We believe that the power to deceive the unsaved intensified 3 decades ago when Maitreya "descended and introduced himself to mankind through Benjamin Creme.

How was Maitreya able to do this? In the one of the most significant scriptures concerning the coming of the anti-Christ, the Apostle Paul warned us through his word to the Thessalonians: " For the mystery of lawlessness is already at work: only He who now restrains will do so until He is taken out of the way. (II Thes: 2: 1-12) Most bible scholars agree that Paul was referring to the Holy Ghost. A few others have suggested that Paul was referring to the fall of the Roman Empire. We are inclined to accept that in this case, the majority has provided the correct interpretation.

Using the life of our founder as a barometer, it is important to note that Pastor Pam has been in Christ since March 29, 1977, less than 3 months prior to Maitreya's visitation to Benjamin Crème. After 31 years, she believes that the Holy Ghost has been restrained at least 3 decades, possibly longer. According to Pastor Pam, the Holy Ghost certainly has not left the elect of God but she perceives that He has been held back within the organized church so that Satan could have his way. In her own words:

> *It is amazing, a true miracle from God that I got saved. Already a willing channel or medium, the Holy Ghost actually stole me out of Maitreya's hands by compelling me with the cross and the resurrection of Jesus Christ of Nazareth.*

Ironically, what was in Pastor Pam's favor was her atheism, for she had no religion and had not been raised in church. So when the religious demon assigned to her channeled pages and pages of writings on Buddhism, Islam and Hinduism and mentioned the "one world religion," she was bored to tears, in no way "interested." Actually, even her carnality was in her favor because all she wanted "the spirits" to reveal to her in those days was "who will be my next boyfriend?"

So when Pam got born again on Monday, March 29, 1977 at 4pm, she had already been a channel to demon spirits from 1974 until that momentous, life changing day. Channeling is a synonym for mediumistic activity. In other words, like Benjamin Creme, Pastor Pam was also a psychic medium, communicating with cosmic beings unknown to her as fallen angels---first with a ouija board and then through automatic writing. In her own words:

> I also saw a few spirit manifestations. By 1977, I had graduated to automatic writing, which is what the channels of today are doing. The final stage of my channeling came when the demon actually stepped into me, pushed my spirit aside, grabbed my larynx and spoke through my mouth, while my spirit stood on the opposite side of the room, jumping up and down yelling, "let me back in. Let me back in." Consequently, the demons who were assigned to "transform me into a channel" in the early 70's were not as skillful as Maitreya was with Benjamin Creme.

> In my case, the Holy Ghost "was not restrained," and He stepped in and literally pulled me out of the religious demon's hands. No one can stop God with those He has called and elected to salvation. No one. Even though the Holy Ghost has been restrained within the organized church, He has still converted, saved and delivered individual sheep. However, with Maitreya's entrance into the earth's sphere, the Holy Ghost has stood back because "Satan's time is short" and he has been given an opportunity as "the god of this world" to touch the elect, just as the Lord removed the hedge from Job.

So while the Holy Ghost has been restrained but not removed, Maitreya has boldly taken credit for a number of world events over the last 30 years. Is the fact that so many counterfeit rebirth experiences have occurred within the organized church in the last 3 decades due to Maitreya's appearing in 1977? Is the fact that the tremendous growth and influence of the word of faith, charismatic movement has occurred in the last 30 years a mere coincidence? And as the charismatic church has increased, the Protestant denominations have subsequently decreased, both in membership, in spiritual power and in influence. Did the unknown and secretive appearance of Maitreya to the earth's atmosphere have a great impact on the present condition of the organized church? We believe so.

THE JEZEBEL SPIRIT: Who it REALLY is!

Yet the plan for Maitreya's entrance was first established through the Jezebel spirit of two women: Helen Blavatsky in 1875 and Alice Bailey from 1919-1949. Both of these women claimed to have received their information telepathically from one or more of the ascended masters. Theosophy is a fragment of the ancient, once universal, wisdom teaching. The masters of Theosophy, located in Tibet and around the world, preserve and extend this ancient wisdom. Periodically they sent forth one of their own - a messenger - to help spread their teachings to all of humanity. In the 1800's they had been searching for a century for the next messenger and finally settled upon Helena Blavatsky, born to a noble Russian family. We would not be surprised if the Blavatsky family were not also members of the Illuminati. We report this kind of history so that you the reader can come to realize just how long plans have been laid. Hopefully, you can get a sense of where we are located within the spiritual time clock of endtime events.

In regards to Blavatsky, she claimed to have seen the master,ie. the fallen angel who would be her teacher in her dreams as a child. She met him in Hyde Park in London when she was 20. She managed to enter Tibet and was trained by those masters in Tibet from 1868 to 1870. From 1875 through her death in 1891 she spread that message around the world. Theosophy is the name Blavatsky gave to that portion of knowledge that she brought from the masters to the world. It comes from the term "Theosophia" used by the Neoplatonists to mean literally "knowledge of the divine". Perhaps all of Blatvatsky's work can be summed up in one of her maxims: Compassion is the law of laws. She explained that brotherhood is not a mere ideal - it is a fact in nature on the spiritual plane. Through the writings of Benjamin Creme, Maitreya and Blavatsky are sending forth the same message.---a concern for humanity.

The Jezebel spirit of Alice Bailey led her to be called "the Mother of the New Age Movement." On June 30, 1895 at the age of fifteen, Bailey had a memorable experience which she reports:

> *"I was sitting in the drawing room reading. The door opened and in walked a tall man dressed in European clothes...but with a tall turban on his head.... He told me there was some work that it was planned that I could do in the world but that it would entail my changing my disposition very considerably;"*

In 1915, Bailey was introduced to Theosophy and the practices of Helena Blavatsky. Through her studies of Blavatsky's Secret Doctrines, Bailey came to believe that the "being" she met at age 15 was Master KH (Koot Hoomi). Prior to her studies ,Bailey had believed that the being she served was the Master Jesus,. Regarding her channeling experiences with this fallen angel, Alice Bailey commented:

> *"I remain in full control of my senses of perception...*
> *. I simply listen and take down the words that I hear and register the thoughts which are dropped one by one into my brain.... I have never changed anything that the Tibetan has ever given to me.... I do not always understand what is given. I do not always agree. But I record it all honestly and then discover it does make sense and evokes intuitive response."*

Bailey spent the majority of her years working out what she referred to as "The Plan." As a result of her works, many other groups were either birthed or influenced. In accord with her theosophical predecessor Blavatski, Bailey also proposed a message of "world peace," the divinity of all mankind, the unity of all religions, and service to mankind. Once a Sunday School teacher and a missionary worker,

Bailey is was renowned by occultists as a prolific author of mystical writings. She actually served as a forerunner to Benjamin Creme, a woman who paved the way to Maitreya .Consequently, Benjamin Creme's perspectives about Maitreya, the world teacher and the other ascended masters were derived from and continue the Theosophical teachings of these two Jezebelian women.

The Jezebel Spirit has been busy for the entire 20th century, preparing for the abomination of desolation when Maitreya will assume fully his role as Satan's angel, when the beast is worshiped around the world as "the Christ." This is how it will be done. Maitreya will not take some man made seat in a building made by man, not the Rock of the Dome or any church building. He has to imitate Jesus Christ of Nazareth and take up his worshipping seat inside temples not made with hands.

Creme also has revealed that when Maitreya declares himself openly to the entire world, when he is accepted by the media to present his credentials, he will mentally overshadow all of humanity simultaneously. Maitreya will come into telepathic rapport with each individual in the world, and each individual will hear him inward, silently, in their own language, as if he were speaking directly to them, which in fact, he will not be.

What will actually happen is that those who have succumbed to passivity, have practiced yoga, tm, chanting, channeling, "speaking in their prayer language" and the like, shall be moved on by the religious demon that is assigned to them. I have wondered why so many professing Christians are able to hear voices, and yet they do not suffer from schizophrenia or any other mental disorder, yet they are constantly tormented by demons. It is all a part of the master plan put in place by Maitreya and his demonic troops worldwide.

Like a cheap but clever magician, Maitreya will appear to be both omnipresent and omniscient through the help of demons who serve him. As a result of this worldwide supernatural occurrence, people will worship Maitreya as "the Christ," and the abomination of desolation shall be fulfilled, according to the scripture. The anti-Christ will be seated in his temple and all the world shall worship him, taking both his seal and his number.

Not so for the elect. Maitreya's telepathic voice shall not be heard by those of us who know the truth, and even if we DO hear, the voice of a stranger we WILL NOT FOLLOW!!!

CHAPTER FOUR

History Repeats Itself!

A common thread throughout the bible from Genesis to Revelation is the ministry of the priesthood. Today, priesthood is understood from the narrow perspective of Roman Catholicism, but a biblical priest is someone who is totally separated from the world in order to serve God. The first known priest was Melchezedec in Abraham's day. After the chosen people came out of Egypt, God told the children of Israel that they would be priests, a holy nation. (Ex 19:6) Simply put, God chose the entire nation of Israel to be His priests. However, after the incident of the golden calf, God limited the priesthood to one of the 12 tribes, the tribe of Levi or the Levites.

From the days of Moses until the Days of Christ on earth, there remained two groups of people in the nation of Israel: the people and the priests. None but the priests could offer sacrifices until Jesus went to the cross and made the final sacrifice of His own blood. So for about 1500 years, no one could come to God directly without the intercession of the priests. Those who offered strange fire in Old Testament times were burned to death. Some died when they entered the holy place. Others died when they tried to offer sacrifices to God. For example, Uzzia died when he stretched out his own hand to steady the ark when it tilted.

However, with the coming of the New Testament age, salvation and redemption reached all men through the sacrifice and the resurrection of Jesus Christ: All who are born again can enter the holy place. "You yourselves also, as living stones, are being built up as a spiritual house into a holy priesthood to offer up spiritual sacrifices acceptable to God through Jesus Christ." (I Peter 2:5) Present your bodies unto God as a living sacrifice, holy and acceptable unto God which is your reasonable service.(Romans 12:1) Once again,God's plan remained the same: two groups were established in the church age: The

Holy Ghost and the priests or priesthood.

After the resurrection and ascension of the Lord Jesus, the church had leaders but there was no organized separation between pulpit and pew. There was no problem from the first century up through the third century. Individually, there may have been isolated problems here and there, but as a whole, all who believed on Jesus were priests. They ALL served God. So much so, that they died for their faith in JESUS.

However, when the Roman Empire under Constantine endorsed Christianity, a division set in. For example, people prospered materially and financially from believing in the Lord, solely because they became a fellow believer of the emperor and a brother to Caesar. Jesus had warned to only render to Caesar what was his, but there came a time when the things of Caesar and the things of God were one and the same. An apparent victory for Christianity in that day over wide-scale persecution, a deceptive peace was the beginning of the downfall of the organized church once the martyrdom of the early church was over.

When this worldly shift occurred, many decided to join Christianity. In the fourth century, another significant shift occurred. During this century, many who joined the church were either unbelievers or "somewhat" of a believer. Those who held worldly power in their hands joined the church, with no desire to serve the Lord in the church. So two classes of believers revived as in the days of the golden calf:the ministers and the people of God. The membership attended to worldly affairs while a few offered themselves to spiritual work, a trend that carried down to this present day. Therefore, the present day church is following in the footsteps of the old covenant, where no longer are ALL of God's people His priests. In fact, the organized church is a actually a hierarchy of priests who have elevated themselves among God's people, creating a distinction, a respecter of persons in the house of God.

Clearly, the Father has been after a universal priesthood. For the true Body of Christ is a kingdom of priests, in spite of the fact that the organized church has returned to the old testament model, where there is a distinction between the pulpit ministry and the people of God. As history reveals, our study of church history shockingly uncovers that the organized church has been out of the will of God since the third century. Wow! The church has been in rebellion to the plan of God for a universal priesthood for more than 1700 years!! Understanding this general, basic history gives us some understanding as to how fallen have been able to establish a seat.

Yet, the organized church is still on earth, bigger and grander than ever in this computerized, global world that we find ourselves in at the dawn of the 21st century. We suspect that we are in the last of the 7 churches mentioned by Jesus in the Book of Revelation. In fact, tracing church history, we have been in the church at Laocidea for perhaps close to a century. The Lord is so merciful, so longsuffering to have endured 17 centuries of corruption within the organized church as well as 1500 years of Israel's disobedience.

We believe that the 7 churches mentioned in the book of Revelation represent various chronological, sequential dispensations. The 6th church mentioned--- called the church of Philadelphia--- may have manifested itself in the 15th century with Martin Luther and the Protestant Reformation,---the church age commended by Jesus in Revelation--- but it did not take long for Protestantism to restore a similar hierarchy that Catholicism has reigned in for centuries. Within both the denominations and the non-denominations, there is that same old distinction: The priests and the pew warmers.

Today as yesterday, a small group of people who call themselves the 5 fold ministry are serving the Lord Jesus Christ as a profession, taking tithes and offerings from the pew warmers as these present day Levites prosper in luxury and ease. Consequently, the pew warmers are taught from the pulpit to "bless the man or woman of God" in order to receive a blessing from Him, even though the veil was torn in two at the cross of Jesus Christ. The church today has returned to the style of the Levitical priesthood. Consequently, how could the organized church be the Body of Christ? Good question.

The significance of the tearing of the temple veil at the moment of the Lord's sacrifice of His own body symbolized that the final sacrifice had been made in God's own blood at the cross. Therefore, all can enter the holy of Holies without a priest acting as an intermediary between God and man. Why? As Jesus declared "IT IS FINISHED." No more sacrifices will be received by the Father because His Son's holy sacrifice has satisfied Him. Since the Lord declared "it is finished", the Father considers all who believe on Jesus Christ of Nazereth to be priests and there is no more Levitical priesthood. Today all who believe on Jesus can eat the showbread, serve at the altar, and enter the holy place. Today God says "You can come" but present day Levite preachers are saying, "you can only come through me. Pay me and let me serve God on your behalf."

Those who belong to Christ need to open their eyes and find out what time it is. The clock is ticking at a rapid pace. Jesus has called the church to repent in the book of Revelation for the last 17 centuries, but the churches throughout the ages has not heeded His call. Think of it. The corruption you see in the present day church has been there for 17 centuries. Could we be at "the end of the end?" Has this organized church of today already been judged yesterday, and is it steadily being transformed into Mystery Babylon? Where is the true remnant of Christ, the Lord's holy priesthood of believers?

Where ever you are, you need to rise up. Know that we are living in the Laodicean age, perhaps since the early 1800's. It is really clear. We are all poor, weak, blind, naked and crippled yet we say that we are rich and have need of nothing. Even so, among us there are priests who have already bought gold from Jesus, have already been tried in the fires of tribulation, and whose dross has been removed.

Hopefully, this book will challenge you to stop wasting your time trying to rebuild on the old foundations. After all, who can erect what God has already judged and torn down?

The Way In!

The widespread infestation of the Fake Jesus, first among the occultists and now within the organized church is probably the single most important contribution of the new age movement to the infiltration of a cleverly hidden evil that looks and sounds humanitarian, peaceful and loving. The ascended masters claim to be overseeing the spiritual development of the human race on both an individual level and on a global plane. According to various accounts, there is a distinct hierarchy of fallen angels in operation to build a kingdom for their master Sunat Kamura.

Through consciousness-altering techniques of yoga, transcendental meditation, channeling, chanting, drugs and hypnosis, millions of New Agers have allegedly received visitations from disembodied beings who have masqueraded as benevolent spirits, duping their hosts into believing that they are sent from God to fulfill His Divine Plan. Yet as depicted in the Book of Genesis, it is a more highly favored achievement for a fallen angel to be able to manifest in the flesh as they did in the days just prior to the flood. In the Lord's warnings about the last days just prior to His second coming, Jesus compared the endtimes to "the days of Noah."

Those who follow and support Benny Hinn may not have noticed that he has been wrong in many of his predictions. However, in both his prayers and his prophecies, Hinn has called for the appearances of spiritual entities to "show up" in churches, not as spirits but "manifested in the flesh." If and when this prediction comes to pass, could this be the "abomination of desolation?" Surely, demons are once again trying to take on flesh, not by coming through the door of the womb of a woman as did Jesus, but they are definitely "climbing up" another way---trying to re-play "the days of Noah." The demons that infested the earth in Noah's day are chained in hell yet, there are other high ranking principalities of the air whose ambition it is to be "embodied." We don't doubt that demons with bodies are already dressing up on Sunday, "going to church, speaking in tongues, no less!!"

With new information coming to light almost daily, we have had to adjust the parameters of our own expectations, "down from a 50 year ballpark to the Lord's return in perhaps 10 years, maybe less." So we encourage anyone of you whose life span could include another decade----if you can, STAY ALIVE PLEASE!!!!! Seriously speaking, from time to time, the spirit of death will try to sneak into your dreams at night to get you to "cooperate with dying." When you awake, fight them in prayer.

Since demons have the capacity to imitate and masquerade as "the dearly departed" in dreams and visions, it is also possible that when fallen show up in church, they will work a strange supernatural sign very much like a mass illusion--- that is, these beings will somehow be able to project themselves as real into the minds of those who are open to receiving such information as true. The other alternative is even more in keeping with the Lord's words about the season of His return as like the days of Noah. So if not a mass illusion, then how could a fallen angel "climb up some other way?"

Furthermore, even though every knee shall bow and every tongue shall confess that Jesus Christ of Nazareth is Lord, there are no demons in the Lord's army. On the contrary, the Fake Jesus has a rebellious, tainted army of demons who torment those who have been duped into worshiping the Fake Jesus---demonic thorns in their counterfeit god's own side. Today--- when we cast out a religious demon from a professing Christian, we NOW have a name to work with, which we didn't have before. We call the demon---- "Sananda."

Remember the Lord's words in John 10. Jesus came into the earth by way of the door. The door or "doorway" is the womb of a woman. Yet Jesus warned that the wolf enters the sheepfold in "an illegal way." Furthermore, To be incarnate the right way is to be "born in the flesh" from day one. The Lord Jesus Christ so trusted His

Father, that He made of Himself of no reputation, coming in the form of a man, not even able to feed Himself or clean His own diaper. The Lord's birth in Bethlehem was "the right and holy way."

Not so with demons. For example, demons hate Christmas because we celebrate a supernatural miracle of the human birth of God on earth, a feat that they have never been able to accomplish. God Himself thought it not robbery to be equal with the Father, yet Jesus set aside His glory as Creator and came in the form of a man through the womb of a woman. In their lust after a body, fallen angels try to enter the earth realm "some other way." In recent studies, we discovered that present day mediums believe and claim that various cosmic beings are not always discarnate but at key moments, they have total access to physical bodies. Consider also what a number of new age occultists have described as a very strange but believable phenomenon known as 'Walk-Ins'.

A **"walk in"** is actually a fallen angel who is said to enter the body of someone who went through a near-death experience and was still alive when the demon moved their spirit aside and "took over" both the body and the soul during or after resuscitation. In other words, as the spirit of an accident victim or of a terminally sick person loses the will to live on an operating table and begins to vacate the body, the demon steps in and takes over the dying just moments before their appointment with death. If this is true, with all of the "near death experiences" that have been reported in our lifetime who have been resuscitated, the foundation of a global build-up of true demon possession is already laid. In fact, it is not surprising that literally every "near death survivor" has "come back to life" preaching the false doctrine of universal love and universal religion with no mention of sin, repentance and the cross of Calvary.

Consequently, Satan can manipulate earth events with 'hands-on' experience through the embodiment of some of his demonic troops.

This would also fit the description, in the Book of Revelation (e.g., Rev.9:1-12), of the demon infested conditions on earth prior to the return of the Lord Jesus Christ at the end of the Age -- not to mention those in the time of Noah (Gen.6:1-6; cf. Mt.24:37).The concept of "walk ins" may also be connected to dissociative identity disorder (DID) and other mental health conditions where a very fearful, traumatic event has caused a person to "flee out of body" in order to cope with horrendous circumstances. The flight of the human spirit in moments of great and sudden terror and fear may very well provide yet another doorway for the embodiment of a discarnate demon. Rape, horrendous accidents, brutalities, torture, horrors of war, to name a few.

So what happens to the spirit of the one who has lost the will to live at his or her death bed once the "walk-in" WALKED IN???? Pam Sheppard's occult experience as a former psychic medium may provide a clue. Before the Holy Spirit rescued her and led her to the cross, she experienced a supernatural phenomena a handful of times in the early 70's that can only be understood through our recent research on the so-called "embodiment" of fallen angels concerning the "walk-ins." Described in all three of her books, the best description is in her first book, "To Curse the Root:"

> *"I did not think a thought or take an action without consulting my spirit guides. As time passed, the style of their communication went from Ouija Board, to spiritual writing with a pen or pencil, (channeling), to their coming into my body for about 5 minutes and speaking through my mouth by taking complete control over my larynx."*
>
> *I remember the first time that I was "taken over" or possessed by them. I did not go into a trance. I was fully conscious, but also totally out of control. One day, after an exhaustive session of spiritual writing, I began to feel dizzy and a little*

> *weak. There was a tugging feeling in my throat. Suddenly, my spirit vacated my body and stood on the opposite side of the room, listening to a conversation that others were having about me. As I stood outside of myself, I can remember thinking, "what in the world is going on here! Let me back into my body." (pg. 26)*

So since the captive to a "walk-in" has not actually died, his or her spirit is lingering on the outside. Weakened for a particular length of time, due to passivity brought about by a death wish, the captive can only return to his or her body when released by "the walk in." Given an awareness of supernatural evil, whether or not we accept the 'Walk-Ins' theory -- it is evident that extraordinary signs are taking place. If the rulers of the darkness of this world are now appearing in a physical body, it would appear to give credence to the fact that the aims of the Ascended Masters are being implemented on the earth today. The goal? A Universal Church that denies the cross, desensitizes sin and the need of the Savior, preaches selfhood and "breakthrough", and a universal world order as it lifts up what the occultists refer to as "the Christ Consciousness"--- a bunch of mumbo jumbo.

So as in the days of Noah, spiritual wickedness in the heavenlies has come to earth. Who knows if we may not already be entertaining "fallen", unaware. So be ye also ready not to be deceived when folk come to you with "come see Jesus in the flesh over here or come see an angel in the flesh over there." We hope that this book is a wake up call to the elect because there are numerous signs to suggest that the ascended masters have been secretly working within the organized church since around 1830. This book will trace how it all began in order to assess where we stand today.

ST. GERMAIN

This demon is particularly "interesting" because he claims to be a "human" god in that he alleges to have been reincarnated several times before he obtained "his divinity." Before Pastor Pam got born again, she had a background with reincarnation:

> *Let me explain to you about reincarnation. When I was an occultist, I was a believer in past lives. However, once I got saved, it was the very first occult belief that I immediately discarded. For anyone who knows the gospel of Jesus Christ realizes that "it is appointed unto man only ONCE to die." As a mere baby Christian, I reasoned to myself, "if my soul could live again in another body to "work out its salvation" with yet another or even several chances to do so, then what was the purpose of Jesus Christ's sacrificial death on the cross?" So I dropped reincarnation like a hot potato.*
>
> *Yet, when I was an occultists, demons disguised in dreams sent me messages that I was the reincarnation of one of my paternal ancestors. To make a long story short, I was given true past family history in an outstanding dream. Later the very same day, my great aunt Irene actually confirmed my dream by revealing the family tree. In my family on my father's side in Antigua existed a white slave master named John who married his slave on her deathbed, Janey Warner, after having sired 15 children with her,--- one of which was my grandfather's father.*

The devil knows how to substantiate a supernatural so called "word of knowledge." His intent is to entrap his targets to receive a lie through what we Christians hold dear----what we have labeled "confirmation." So he "confirmed" reincarnation due to the fact that I received actual ancestral information in a supernatural way, substantiated by my great aunt. Once I accepted the "confirmation" ---don't start laughing---I began to believe that I was the reincarnation of my great, great grandfather John--a white slave holder who married his slave. Since as a black woman who at that very time was dating a white man, I was convinced that I was working out some kind of karma carried over from my past life. Yes, I am able to admit that I used to be quite the idiot so if you are laughing at me right now, I wonder if you too have some real foolish stuff hid away in your own closet along with the skeletons!!!

In all seriousness, before Pastor Pam was saved, she had ended up believing in reincarnation so strongly, that she began to conduct past life hypnosis with anyone who would be her guinea pig which was usually either a friend or a family member. Well, she seriously snapped out of this practice when one of her past life regressions went sour and "refused to come back." That's right. Pastor Pam took a friend back into the womb and then "beyond" into 3 different so-called past lives with 3 different names and identities. She was in for a very rude awakening.

When she started the count down for the comeback to close out the hypnotic trance, the demon (she didn't know it was a demon back then) began to mock her by mimicking her. As she closed out with, "5, 4, 3,---coming back, opening your eyes," the demon repeated her very words in a "sing song" tone through her friend's mouth and refused to let her friend go." Panicked, Pastor Pam leaped out of her seat, grabbed her friend and shook her until she woke up. When her friend "came to, the woman had no idea what had transpired, nor any remembrance of the 3 entities. Yet she looked at the wall and saw some handwriting on it that Pastor Pam could not see. There was a message written there to her by one of her so called "past lives." When the friend read the names of the 3 entities, Pastor Pam was flabbergasted. She was correct. So after this incident in the 70's, Pastor Pam did no more past life regressions.

So what ACTUALLY DOES happen to convince people that reincarnation is real? There is a rather simple explanation. The demons that are on earth now were here since BEFORE Adam and Eve were created. So they know everyone who has ever lived, including the details of their lives. Like magicians, they can even materialize on occasion, usually at someone's deathbed or in dream. In the movie the Exorcist, the demon who possessed the girl was able to imitate the voice of the priest's mother and work on his conscience for not having been a dutiful son while she was alive. Demons often are assigned to families and they know everyone, generations past. It is a small matter to reveal to a psychic or a medium information concerning the past histories of anyone---including details.

With this same principal and pattern, a demon can provide information to a medium relative to a crime that was committed, a hidden object, etc. The demon was there not only invisibly watching and "takin notes", but doing everything within its power to make the crime happen. Demons also know where objects are hidden. How? Well the demon was either there itself or one of its cohorts sent it the information through telepathic communication between demons within our atmosphere. Just as we have telephones and we can send messages anywhere in the world through the airways, demons have their own unearthly means of communication.

So since we know that reincarnation is a lie, St. Germain seems to be the biggest liar of all of the ascended masters put together for he declares that he is the reincarnation of a host of human beings who lived in different generations. Interestingly enough, included in this long list of past lives is the Prophet Samuel and Joseph, the surrogate father of Jesus Christ. Yet, to have been so significantly "embodied", it seems rather a significant drop in spiritual attainment to then claim to be the reincarnation of Plato and a host of Greeks and Romans. He also claims to have lived as Roger Bacon from 1220-1292, an English educational reformer renowned for his exhaustive investigations into mathematics and languages, as well as Francis Bacon of the 16th century--another English philosopher and statesman.

Yet what is noteworthy about Germain as an ascended master is his American influence as portrayed in his claiming a past life as the reincarnation of Christopher Columbus and his boasting that the nickname "Uncle Sam" is referring to him. Now, granted, Germain is merely a demon in masquerade. He was probably assigned to monitor the lives of those human beings that he appears to "know so well" and falsely claims to have "embodied." Perhaps Germain had moments when he was actually able to enter some of them, certainly not the prophet Samuel or Joseph, but I wouldn't doubt if he didn't enter into some of those Greeks and Romans from time to time.

Nevertheless, what causes us to pay serious attention to Germain's influence is that he also boasts to his occult followers of having been the father of freemasonry. History reveals that practically all of the founding fathers of this country were freemasons. The dollar bill boasts the symbols of this Luciferean secret society. Yet another of the many proofs of Freemasonry's deep influence upon the American culture and mentality is the Statue of Liberty. This colossal statue was fashioned after the goddess Ishtar. Ishtar was the ancient Sumero-Babylonian goddess of love and fertility. The statue was conceived by Freemasons, financed by Freemasons, built by Freemasons, and installed by Freemasons in a masonic ceremony. The maker of the statue was Freemason Frederic-Auguste Bartholdi.Therefore, the demon who calls himself "St. Germain" may very well be central to the founding of America in the New World.

So as I surveyed through endless writings that emanated from Germain's channels, I have tried to uncover his real, sinister purpose. Throughout the pages and pages of channeled written communications, there is a general agreement among occultists that Germain is the father of what they call "the Golden Age." " Students of the ascended master teachings---particularly the many who channel messages from Germain--- believe that this world is destined to again have a Golden Age, a "Heaven on Earth", that will be permanent, unlike previous Golden Ages. Most of Germain's channels have received the following message:

> "In your beloved America, in the not so far distant future, will come forth a similar recognition of the Real Inner Self, and this her people will express in high attainment. She is a Land of Light, and Her Light shall blaze forth, brilliant as the sun at noonday, among the nations of the Earth. She was a Land of Great Light, ages ago, and will again come into her spiritual heritage, for nothing can prevent it." "The Divine Plan for the future of North America is a condition of intense activity in the greatest peace, beauty, success, prosperity, spiritual illumination, and dominion. She is to carry the Christ Light and be the Guide for the rest of the Earth, because America is to be the Heart Center of the 'Golden Age' that is now dimly touching our horizon. The greater portion of the land of North America will stand for a very long time.""In your beloved America, in the not so far distant future, will come forth a similar recognition of the Real Inner Self, and this her

people will express in high attainment. She is a Land of Light, and Her Light shall blaze forth, brilliant as the sun at noonday, among the nations of the Earth. She was a Land of Great Light, ages ago, and will again come into her spiritual heritage, for nothing prevent it. She is strong within her own mind and body stronger than you think; and that strength she will exert to rise out of, and throw off   from border to border, all that weighs heavily upon her at the present time.

"America has a destiny of great import to the other nations of the Earth, and Those who have watched over her for centuries still watch. Through Their protection and Love, she shall fulfill that destiny. America! We, the Ascended Host of Light, love and guard you. America! We love you.

> "A similar form of perfect government will come at a later period, when you have cast off certain fetters within that hang like fungi, and sap your strength as a vampire. Beloved ones in America, be not discouraged, when the seeming dark clouds hang low. Every one of them shall show you its golden lining. Back of the cloud that seems to threaten, is the "Crystal Pure Light of God and His Messengers, the Ascended Masters of Love and Perfection" watching over America, the government, and her people. Again I say, "America, we love you."

Such rhetoric is rather scary when you consider that it sounds very much like the preaching of mega ministers, particularly in the area of dominion theology. Certainly, we have all wondered as to the role of America in endtime events. In some interpretations of various symbols in the book of Daniel and Revelation, some eschatologists do not even mention America which has a sinister suggestion that the nation is destroyed before the end of the tribulation. In actual fact, there is no nation on this earth that can compare to our strength, might and power---at least not since the fall of the Soviet Union. Let's not forget the Roman Empire, as "it is no more!"

Nevertheless, we believe that no other stage in history has the scene been so fully set for the manipulation of a deception of global proportions through the instrumentality of these fallen demons that call themselves "ascended masters". For the situation in which we find ourselves today is more bizarre and far-reaching than the most imaginative science fiction novel. The age of Aquarius ended in the year 2000, and now the occultists declare the world has entered an era known as "the Golden Age." Germain holds the stature of being the leader or "god of the Golden Age." As countless people are tuning into and receiving instructions from demons masquerading as benefactors and helpers, deception is clearly rampant,--- as out of control as a runaway train, headed in any inconceivable direction. Whatever conclusion we may reach, the deception is clearly satanic because of the occultic and "anti-Christ" direction in which those under its influence have been subsequently led.

After careful consideration of various segments of Germain's channeled material that we have reviewed, we find that the entire charade is being masterminded by Satan in opposition to God, as part of a global build-up to the founding of a demonic view of 'kingdom' on earth. The title 'ascended master' has been used deliberately by the powers of darkness to challenge the uniqueness of the Lord Jesus and to usurp His unrivaled status. We have the Lord's own word for it that 'No one has ascended to heaven but He who came down from heaven, that is, the Son of Man who is in heaven' (Jn.3:13). Germain and the rest of them are certainly in no way 'ascended', but have rather "descended" from the heavenlies that surround the earth and even higher, from the second heaven where the other planets consist.

It is beyond the scope of this book to examine each and every way that the demon called "Germain" and his depiction of the Golden Age has infiltrated each and every church doctrine and practice, for we perceive that his influence is too far reaching for that. For example, as noted above, Germain claims to be the founder of freemasonry and perhaps one day, we will do some research and prepare some written material on the subject. In "Faces of the Religious Demon," Pastor Pam writes about the ramifications of the infiltration of freemasonry in the African American church and the backlash of destruction that tends to fall on the families of Christian members of the masonic lodge.

However, another rather outstanding "Golden Age, " Germain-type influence is Dominion Theology. Much of today's apostolic emphasis has connections to dominion theology. Not easily attached to any particular segment within the organized church, dominion teaching has crossed several lines and has diversified applications. Yet the one central thought is an endtime issue---that Jesus Christ CANNOT or WILL NOT come back to earth until the church has taken control of at least a significant portion of earth's political and social institutions. Such a theology goes beyond Germain and moves up the demonic hierarchy to both Sananda and Maitreya. The Germain influence is that of man's self actualization in his personal pursuit of freedom toward attainment of his "Christed state of divinity." In other words, if every man develops his "Christ consciousness within", then the subtle apostasy that under girds a search for individual freedom is that "Christ as we know Him, need not return at all."

So that you see the connection, here are some quotations from one of the leading proponents of Dominion Theology, Earl Paulk, the Pastor of Chapel Hill Harvest Church in Atlanta Ga. It is unclear if this is the Sr. or the Jr. The "junior" is the one who has been in the news concerning various well publicized sex scandals. Read Paulk's words:

"Christ IN US must take dominion over the earth. The next move of God CANNOT occur until Christ IN US takes dominion. Christ was one person, limited to ministry in only one place at a time. In order to minister as an omni-present Spirit, Jesus relinquished his fleshly dimension with its limitations of time and place. He entered a realm of restoration and love by becoming an indwelling spirit."

Now how does Paulk's words differ from that channeled by Germain?

We don't see much difference!!!

"One by one, great awakened souls are coming forth who will become clearly conscious of their own mighty, inherent God-Power, and such as these will be placed in all official positions of the government. They will be more interested in the welfare of America than in their own personal ambitions and private fortunes. Thus, will another Golden Age reign upon earth, and be maintained for an aeon."

CHAPTER FIVE

An Angelic Conspiracy Theory

In the last 50 years or so, we have become overwhelmed by the interpretations of a plethora of self proclaimed endtime prophecy bible scholars. The problem with many "endtime watchers" is that their understanding of symbolic scriptures is just too complicated for the masses to understand. We believe that the Lord is about "simplicity." In fact, when the time is at hand, the symbols of the old testament and the book of Revelation shall be simple to translate even for the babes in Christ among us. Once the actual events begin to unfold, the symbols will be easy to understand "in hind sight."

Simply put, we do not need to rummage through newspapers, nor is it necessary to keep an account of current events to determine when a man made temple will be built in the middle east on the Rock of the Dome, nor do we need to keep a daily account of potentially prophetic occurrences in Israel and the middle east. Perhaps a temple will actually be built. However, the bible suggests in some key scriptures that the day of worship in a man-made temple is "over." Since the finished work of the Lord at the cross bore witness in the tearing down of the veil of the Jewish temple, the Lord's final words have told the tale"---- IT IS FINISHED!!! Temple worship in a man-made shrine is OVER! Since the cross, God's temple is the human heart. Satan wants to be worshiped in God's temple!!!

In truth, the elect must not depend upon these "book of revelation" specialists, with particular skepticism toward those who believe in an idyllic escape of the church in a pre-tribulation rapture. The rapture as it is taught is an insult to so many faithful martyrs who gave up their lives for Jesus Christ in other generations. Was their sacrifice for the sake of lukewarm, meely mouthed, self centered "bless me Jesus" professing Christians who simply desire to "escape?"

No, such a scenario just doesn't cut it with our understanding of the scriptures . Clearly, we are in the last church age of "Laodicea." Other than for the remnant, how can lukewarm believers deserve such a blessing? Moreover, how can even the remnant "overcome," unless we "go through" the tribulation in victory? Good questions indeed. A true believer will either die a natural death, the death of a martyr or overcome and live until Jesus comes again.

The Beast and the False Prophet

Other than for "the dragon," practically every interpretation of Revelation and other endtime scriptures automatically assumes that the two beasts---the anti-Christ and the false prophet---are human beings. This may very well be the case. However, consider both the king and the prince of Tyre in Ezekiel 28. The human ruler of Tyre was a flesh and blood actual human prince, yet the "king of Tyre" was the highest ranking fallen angel, the devil himself. Since Satan is still the god of this world, we should expect that behind every political position, an invisible demon reigns. Not to suggest that every politician or even every pope is demonized, but cleverly hidden behind the scenes of both politics and the papacy is a political demon who rules "politically" and a religious demon who rules "religiously."

Surely, if Maitreya is the anti-Christ, he intends to be embodied at some key point in time. Some believe that the anti-Christ will "come in the flesh" of a European ruler. Others point their prophetic fingers at a USA President. I want to emphasize here that I personally do not have a clue who the human being may be. What I am confident of is that when I hear his voice, I will know him by "his rap." To know Satan's agenda is to know the anti-Christ. Those who serve Maitreya in the flesh cannot restrain themselves from speaking forth his agenda. That is their "calling" and they can't help but declare it.

Consider the two Jezebelians, **Helen Blavatski** and **Alice Bailey**. Both women of different centuries consistently sent forth

Maitreya's message in accord with his present day "best man", Benjamin Creme. In keeping with this unified platform, Maitreya meets every condition of the spirit of the anti-Christ. If there is an actual flesh and blood leader, he or she will declare Maitreya's platform both in politics and in religion. Therefore, in order to spot the anti-Christ, you have to know "his platform." If you assume that Satan's platform is always evil and negative, you are already deceived.

Generally, a Hollywood or made for TV "who done it" will point to several possible suspects who are "more or less obvious." With mystery movies, the least obvious character is very often the murderer. Consider one of my favorite movies, "the Pelican Brief" starring Julia Roberts and Denzel Washington. . Roberts plays the lead character, Darby Shaw, a young law student. As somewhat of an intellectual prank, Darby Shaw puts together a brief, a kind of conspiracy theory to impress her law professor, as to who was behind the assassination of two supreme court justices---fictionalized, of course.

Running rings around the investigations of the professionals in the CIA and the FBI, Darby's strategy was very "simple." She centered on commonalities and motive. Darby discovered that the two assassinated justices held different voting patterns and opinions on every case that came before them. However, there was one commonality. In one case, both justices voted to protect the environment relative to an endangered species of pelicans. If the two justices had lived, a huge oil company would lose billions of dollars if their appeal was denied.

This one element of commonality led to the culprit--an oil magnet named Mattice-- a very close friend of the sitting president ofthe USA. With two vacated spots on the Supreme Court's bench, Mattice was "confident" that his friend, the President, would choose two justices sympathetic to his plight. However, the President's term was about to expire and his running for a second term was doubtful. Once the President was out of office, Mattice could not risk taking a chance on the choice of an unknown, future president. Therefore, Darby Shaw hit the nail on the head. Only one commonality led to motive, motive led to fact and the truth was "obvious." A young law student broke a conspiracy theory wide open.

In like manner, our study of Maitreya is like "breaking a conspiracy theory" in a search for commonality and motive. What hinders the breaking of the code's mystery is a lack of knowledge of Satan and the underlying issues of his fall and his rebellion toward God in the first place. Right now, Satan is still "the god of the world" and "the prince of the powers of the air" only because God has allowed it. Our God has always been and still is in complete control. Simply put, God has permitted fallen Lucifer to remain the invisible force behind all nations and systems of both man and of fallen angels because our God has a plan.

Actually, fallen angels are MORE under the thumb of Satan's power than are human beings because of our free will. Since we have the God given right to choose, even God Himself does not control us. Consequently , before he can dominate and control us, Satan has to FIRST deceive us. Once we fall into his trap, then we "are his." This one "spiritual fact" is the cornerstone of our "conspiracy theory." Satan can control demons better than he can exercise his power to control us. Consequently, in Satan's last hour, it stands to reason that he'd prefer to depend on a high ranking demon as the anti-Christ than an unpredictable human being.

You may be surprised at this but human beings without Christ are children of wrath, rebellion and disobedience who refuse to obey not only God, but man is rebellious against other men, himself as well as the devil. Surely, our affinity toward sin can lead us to descend to evil, as we ignorantly become an adopted child of Satan. Yet we are not by nature "satanists." We are "humanists" devoted to ourselves in our pursuit of pleasure and happiness." Even faithful followers of Satan had to be tricked into embracing devil worship. Here are excerpts from Pam's testimony. taken from website articles:

"When I consider my own old unregenerate self as an atheist, I was foolishly confident in my own "goodness." As such, I was not interested in serving either God, man or the devil, because I was my only god. As I did not believe in God's existence, I also did not believe that a being actually existed called Satan. In truth, I would never have even touched the occult, it I thought that the devil was involved, so demons had to first lure me by seduction, deceive me by flattery and then entrapped me in a spiritual web from which I could not escape without the intervention of the Holy Ghost. Yet God Himself, though silent for a time, was always in complete control. Even though I sought to be "empowered" with great passion, fearlessness and zeal to communicate with "the other side," , my psychic powers were purposefully "limited."

For example, I sat for hours at a time, calling out to my spirit guide"s," yet they did not come even one time when I called for them. Even though I fervently lusted after the power of telepathy, the demons were never able to communicate to me "mind to mind." They could take my hand and move it across a Ouija board and even use a pen in my hand to scroll across a piece of paper, but even that was limited. I could not "write" unless someone else was holding the top of the pen.

They were also able to vacate my spirit, even step into me, but only a handful of times for just a few minutes. On a few occasions, I heard voices, only the voices were not "in" me but outside of me. As much as I wanted to be a "fortune teller," I was too honest to "fake it." True psychics have the spirit of divination inside their own spirit, speaking to them regularly and consistently. Because of this "inward telepathic communication, fortune tellers and other prognosticators are able to "read a person." Without a consistent telepathic stream of communication, I was forced to prognosticate only through astrology. I can look back more than 3 decades and be "real" in my thanksgiving and praise of God for the limits and boundaries that he set to protect me.

Furthermore, in spite of my flesh inclinations toward the spirit of Jezebel, without strong limits on the religious demon, I could have been on a par with Helen Blavatsky, Alice Bailey and Benjamin Creme. In fact, the demons frequently promised me in their automatic writings of their goal for my future--- to train me to be a psychic on the level of an Edgar Cayce or a Jean Dixon. Once I got saved, it never happened, praise God. The miracle of my salvation experience was brought home to me in early 2008. While shopping in Walmart, I was stunned to be recognized without hesitation by a 45 year old man who accosted me:

> *"You don't recognize me, Pam? Well, I guess you don't cause I was just a kid. You did my astrology chart and that of all the kids in the neighborhood. " He recognized me after 33 years without a blink of an eye. I quickly smiled, but shook my head with, "oh, I don't do astrology charts anymore." I'm sure his memory was correct but my own memory of doing the*

> *whole neighborhood's astrology chart is so vague, that it is practically wiped out. I realized standing in Walmart, that I am indeed "a new creation" and that there is no condemnation to those who are in Christ Jesus."*

We suspect that it is easier for Satan to control and manage fallen angels than human beings. Due to the intricate requirements that full scale deception and seduction entail as well as the limits that God Himself sets on Satan where it comes to His elect, Satan's job is not as easy as we might expect. Moreover, due to our multiplicity of social and ethnic groupings, as a species, human beings have countless conflicting desires and agendas. Therefore, issues of self interest lead to clashing wills in our everyday struggle to uplift all kinds of opposing agendas. To further interfere with Satan's overall agenda, the demons themselves have different areas of responsibility that often conflict with other groups of demons.

Take the abortion issue as a simple example. Under the domain of the spirit of death known in scripture as "the death angel", there are demons who specialize in killing fetuses. Yet on the opposite side are "other" demons who use anti-abortion zealots to bomb clinics. So one military company of demons lines up against another company with a clashing agenda on two opposing sides---those who kill for "pro-choice" and pro-lifers who kill by assaulting pro-abortionists. In any major issue, there will be demons opposing each other on several sides of the equation, as they attempt to kill, steal and destroy.

So Satan's army is often at odds with each other over priorities and targets of spiritual warfare. The Lord Jesus revealed that from the days of John the Baptist, Satan's kingdom suffered violence, as his demonic forces became divided against themselves. Charismatic interpretations have suggested that God's kingdom suffered violence, but actually it is Satan's kingdom that suffered violence with the preaching of repentance. From that point on, Satan has failed to unify his own spiritual forces.

So who are "the violent who take it by force?" We suspect that "the violent" are the strongest in the battle, whether they be God's or Satan's demons. We can comprehend the nature of a spiritual battle by studying Daniel Chapter 10. An angel was bringing an answer to prayer to Daniel, when the angel was delayed by opposing demons. The angel declared to Daniel, "The prince of the kingdom of Persia withstood me for 21 days,and behold, Michael, one of the chief princes, came to help me for I had been left alone there with the kings of Persia." So Jesus declared that from the preaching of John the Baptist, the violence between angelic beings would increase.

In the midst of spiritual militarism, Satan has reserved the Ascended Masters--- the devil's final "big guns,"--- cosmic beings of great power and intelligence. In this regard, Satan's final stand before he is thrown into the lake of fire is to mobilize his highest ranking generals to organize and rule the world before the return of Jesus Christ of Nazareth---in his final effort to prove that the world does not need the real Jesus.

As the Master of Masters, Maitreya is Satan's top "endtime player" whose job is to bring order to the chaos of this planet by establishing a regime based on brotherhood. This is Maitreya's "rap." Through Benjamin Creme and others, Maitreya's motives seem too pure and unselfish to be connected to Satan, and there lies the power behind the deception. Not only the lost of the world but even some of the elect will not suspect that the elimination of racism, poverty, starvation, unity, and sharing for the common good could possibly have its roots underlying Satan's ultimate agenda. With this kind of positive rhetoric, the devil is portrayed in the mystery of Maitreya as "the least likely culprit."

Another inconsistent element is that Maitreya plans to call on the help of man to fulfill his noble goals. We all have witnessed in our times and throughout world history that man is certainly capable of good and worthy acts. Consider the well televised media coverage that immediately followed the falling of the twin towers of the World Trade Center in NYC on 9/11/01. Who was not touched by the crowds of people roaming downtown New York, holding up pictures of their missing relatives and the acts of human kindness generated not only within the city, but throughout the nation and the world?

Obviously, this horrendous terrorist attack was inspired by demons, without a doubt. Yet the good that came out of it was extremely noteworthy. How can we forget the firefighters, the policemen, and several other volunteer rescuers, the churches, the counselors---every world system was affected in a positive way relative to care for the bereaved and the broken city in such wonderful acts of brotherly love. Let's not forget the increase in American patriotism, with emblems of the stars and stripes posted everywhere. It was amazing.

Yet, brotherly love, compassion and support did not last but for a rather short season. The civil lawsuits that have followed depict the true nature of man, with no special emphasis on those who lost their loved ones or their lives in 911. The word of God is clear. The love of money is the root of ALL evil. The sinful, fallen nature of all humans is on accord with that of Satan. Some of the 911 lawsuits are absolutely ridiculous. Unable to sue the terrorists directly, survivors of world trade victims have attempted to sue for everything and anything greedy lawyers can come up with. For example, Arab investments in the USA approximate $750 billion dollars. So any potential financier of terrorism is being sued because the allegation is that "they allowed the event to occur.". Those who inhaled the dust during their heroic efforts to save and rescue lives are also suing. The airlines are being sued because of their apparent mismanagement that "led to the possibility of the hy-jackings in the first place." Such a lawsuit is outrageous!!! Why not sue who ever it was who invented the airplane???!!!! There is even a lawsuit on the books to force a criminal investigation of the President of the USA!!! All too sad yet typical of human nature everywhere in the world.

So if Maitreya expects a full scale cooperation of earth's inhabitants in his efforts toward brotherhood and saving the planet, he is in for a rude awakening! This dilemma must be a great frustration for Satan since he is the one who seduced man's defilement in the first place!!! Satan simply did not anticipate that he would need man at the end to promote his own agenda to "rule the world." The irony is that through deception, Satan lured Adam and Eve into sin. Yet sin is the reason why man can do nothing of permanent "good" and all human goodness and effort of cooperation are doomed.

Surely, there is enough good in man to help people in need but there is no good in man that can satisfy God. Since all humans have sinned and fallen short of God's glory, all human goodness is tarnished beyond repair without the cross. Could Maitreya's future failure to unite mankind result in the second half of the tribulation when he discovers that even with all of his counterfeit miracles and healings, mankind without "the real Christ" will remain stubborn, headstrong and rebellious.? With no answers available yet, we imagine that all hell will break loose. The horror is that the evil works of disgruntled and outraged terrorists shall be as mere child's play by comparison to angelic military warfare.

Hitler had his ovens but what Maitreya has in store for rebells certainly necessitates the return of the Lord to rescue the elect to keep us from perishing in the final hour. Remember. Maitreya is not a man. He is a fallen angel. Angelic torture is beyond our human understanding. At the final hour, the Lord will truly have to step in and save His elect. Before he is thrown into the lake of fire along with Satan, Maitreya will be humiliated when he discovers that only the return of Jesus Christ of Nazareth will bring righteousness and peace to earth.

      Here is another important question to ask as we try to understand the nature of spiritual warfare. What has been Satan's motive, from the beginning of recorded time? There is one basic, biblical, simple answer. Lucifer fell not only because he wants to be like God. Satan wants to BEEEEE God!!!! It is as simple as that. Taken a step further, when we make our feeble attempts to define or to describe God, we say 3 things: He is omnipotent, He is omniscient and He is omnipresent: all powerful, all knowing and everywhere!!! Man may have some skills as a magician, but I'd like to see a Houdini type human being pull something off like what Maitreya proposes to do in the realm of the spirit. Well, with his power and spiritual resources, Maitreya has the capacity to pull off mass telepathy among unbelievers, counterfeit Christians and the deluded among the elect.

CHAPTER SIX

The Plot Thickens!

The way Maitreya plans to "pull it off" shall be achieved through the self imposed passivity of millions, perhaps billions. The key word is "altered states of consciousness." The Ascended Masters have been preparing the souls and spirits of man of each generation "for years." Hindus and Buddhists have been prepared for generations. Those who indulge in witchcraft and its various derivatives are also prepared. The mentally ill and the substance abuser are also open to telepathy.

The last target is "the organized church." Catholicism is already prepared with its idolatrous veneration of saint worship, for the spirits behind the saints are actually "demons." Once again, the Vatican is now supporting that we must embrace extraterrestrial brotherhood. Protestants are being prepared through counterfeit tongues and the phenomena of "slain in the spirit." The plan is that the sheep of earth shall telepathically hear "the voice of a stranger." Unable to rejoice in his apparent victory that detached man from the presence of God, Satan learned early on right there in the garden of Eden that One was coming Who would bruise his head. Therefore much of Satan's activity in the old testament resulted from his attempt to detach the people from God and to attach them to himself. To try and stop his head from being bruised, Satan continued to try to block the first coming of Jesus Christ. Christmas Day was a real blow to him. The Redeemer had come.

Detachment from God is strongly connected to his next strategy--- to attempt to sneakily attach God's people to himself. The detachment-attachment strategy worked when Satan led the Israelites "a whoring" after other gods and idols---gods that were high level fallen angels in Satan's own army. In spite of all of his effort,

Satan's head was ultimately bruised at the cross when the sins of the "lower creature" were forgiven and forgotten in the sacrifice of the Son. The Father chose to "lord it over Satan "by sending His Son in the body of a mere man. So God Himself restored His own creation by redeeming the chosen ones by the sacrifice of His own precious blood.

Today, Satan is re-working the same strategy upon churchfolk and professing Christians: DETACHMENT FROM GOD AND ATTACHMENT TO HIMSELF in countless ways on numerous levels. Take yoga as an example. Some of the clients that we have worked with over the years practiced yoga BEFORE they became a Christian. They are now being tormented. The torment that they are enduring today is unimaginable. The obscenities, cursings, blasphemies and ravings that come forth out of the mouths and throats of those whom Hindu demons control is "unearthly",especially when they also speak in tongues. Deliverance is progressive, but we are experiencing some success.

Christian Yoga

Yoga is rooted in Eastern mysticism, incompatible with Christianity. Yet, there are Christians who believe that it is possible to extract physical benefits from yoga, in spite of its demonic roots. In fact, there is now an acceptable practice, spreading like wild fire primarily in the denominational churches called "Christian Yoga." Operating in some of the United Methodist Churches and the Parkwood Baptist Church, it is believed that "getting quiet to hear God" by "tuning out the world's frequency to tune into God's frequency" is obtainable through Christianized yoga. Church leaders ignorantly believe that applying scripture to yoga provides an opportunity for its participants to receive Jesus Christ as Lord and Savior.

What the deceived do not know is that conversion to Jesus Christ of Nazareth through the practice of yoga is akin to expecting "Satan to cast out Satan." It just won't happen. Why? Because through passivity, yoga stretches wide open the seven psychic centers in the body known in the occult world as chakras. Chakras are actually demonic doorways for Hindu deities who themselves are principalities and powers. Each of these demons rules a particular sphere of life, which we are presently researching. Once these doorways are opened through passivity, the deities stand guard over each portal: Over the crown is Shiva; the third eye is Hakini; the throat is Savashiva, the heart is Isha, the navel is Vahni, the gut is Vishnu and Rakeeni and the anus is Brahma.

The main problem is that the passivity of the yoga practitioner has weakened his will. This kind of passivity empowers any one or all 8 demons or deities. While each deity stands guard over the doorways that it rules, countless other lower demons pass in and out of each of the 7 portals. To unseat a demonic deity is not impossible but it is very challenging, to say the least. What we are presently learning is that once the captive is strong enough in his or her will, each demon must be cast out one at a time by the name of the deity. Then the blood of Jesus Christ of Nazareth must be applied to the doorposts of the 7 psychic centers in order to permanently close these doorways, opened by the apparently harmless practice of yoga.

Almost one hundred years ago, woman of God Jessie Penn Lewis in collaboration with Evangelist Evan Roberts of the revival in Wales wrote a life saving and life changing book entitled "War on the Saints." This book has no competition or comparison. No one has defined passivity better than Jessie Penn Lewis:

> The primary cause of deception and possession in surrendered believers may be condensed into one word, PASSIVITY; that is, a cessation of the active exercise of the WILL in control over the spirit, soul and body or either, as may be the case.
> It is, practically, a counterfeit of "surrender to God." The believer who surrenders his

> members or faculties to God, AND CEASES TO USE THEM HIMSELF, thereby falls into "passivity" which enable evil spirits to deceive, and possess any part of his being which has become passive."
>
> This deception over passive surrender may be exampled thus: A believer surrenders his "arm" to God. He permits it to hang passive, waiting for 'God to use it.' He is asked, 'why do you not use your arm?' He replies, 'I have surrendered it to God. I must not use it now. God must use it.' But will God lift the arm for the man? Nay, the man himself must lift it, and use it, seeking to understand intelligently God's mind in doing so. (War on the Saints, pg. 71.)

Sister Lewis amplified this general definition of passivity as a state of being out of control because of a loss of free will, a condition of inactivity or idleness. In order to know what is going on in the spiritual realm, every serious Christian should have access to "War on the Saints."

Unable to rejoice in his apparent victory that detached man from the presence of God, Satan learned early on right there in the garden of Eden that One was coming Who would bruise his head. Therefore much of Satan's activity in the old testament resulted from his attempt to detach the people from God and to attach them to himself. To try and stop his head from being bruised, Satan continued to try to block the first coming of Jesus Christ. Christmas Day was a real blow to him. The Redeemer had come.

We may be the lower creation in the devil's eyes but Satan knows that it is God's will that the kingdom of darkness be ruled and dominated by those who belong to Jesus Christ of Nazareth. Since Satan's days are short, in view of the closing days of the age of the organized church, demonic onslaughts shall increase. To be defeated by an inferior creation is the greatest humiliation that Satan's kingdom must endure. Yet God Himself has raised us, an inferior creation-- to a status once occupied by Satan when he was the great archangel of God. We are lifted up by our Triumphant Lord, to the place of judgment where "we shall judge ." It is a very humbling experience to "cast out a demon" and have it obey you, simply because you belong to the kingdom of the Christ.

Also, consider this. The words of Jesus as recorded in John 10:1-5 are extremely significant to endtimes. To understand, we must break the symbolic code. To enter the sheepfold by the door is to be born of a woman. Jesus fulfilled this requirement by "taking on flesh", and entering this earth's atmosphere through his human mother, Mary, as He was conceived by the Holy Ghost. How frustrating for Satan that he cannot "be born" as we are, nor can any of his fallen . So as Jesus warns, "they climb up some other way." Who climbs up some other way? Clearly its fallen and demons. They are the thieves and the robbers who are functioning on earth "illegally".

Since spirits, cosmic beings---even the ascended masters---- have no bodies of their own to function on this earth, so they attempt to use "ours." Consequently, the only way Maitreya can obtain a body is to snatch one through a trap set by deception. Maitreya has been gradually "climbing up some other way" since 1875 when he first telepathically communicated to a human being, Helen Blavatsky. He moved into the early to mid 20th century through the apostasy of an Episcopalian woman, Alice Bailey. It took more than a half a century to reach Benjamin Creme. According to Creme, Maitreya is looking forward to the day when all men on earth shall hear his voice in their own language at the same time to prove that Maitreya is "omnipotent, omniscient and omnipresent."

This goal provides yet additional understanding as to the importance of the counterfeit of speaking in other tongues. God

Himself brought forth many languages to the world to hinder the building of the Tower of Babel. In Genesis 11, we read that because of the people's rebellion, God "confused the language of all the earth" so that the people would not be able to understand each other's speech. How ironic and counter-rebellious on the part of Maitreya. Satan's representative in endtimes is looking to do just the opposite in Mystery Babylon, which includes various segments of the organized church: Maitreya's goal is to cause all who speak in different tongues to hear him in ONE tongue, a complete reversal of God's actions to hinder the building of the tower of Babel. This is blasphemy to the nth degree. Anyone who does not close the door to self induced passivity is at risk of becoming reprobate.

To continue with the rest of John 10, Jesus declared that He is the door of the sheep. All who ever came before Him, or proceeded His first coming,----- Jesus calls them both thieves and robbers but the sheep,---the children of Israel---did not receive them as Messiah. Perhaps this scripture also applies to His second coming. However, Maitreya is boldly contradicting the words of Jesus by declaring that he himself is the door of the sheep, that he in fact, is the good shepherd or as Creme calls him "the World Teacher."

Take another look at what Maitreya proposes to do: eliminate starvation, sickness and disease, poverty, racism, bring about universal brotherhood, unity, peace, healing, fair distribution of the world's resources, sharing,---in other words, Maitreya is promising "the abundant life" on earth for everyone. What apparently pure motives!!!! Yet, Maitreya is a hireling. He has already entered earth's atmosphere deceptively and out of order for he cannot be "born of a woman." As the "Master of Masters", Maitreya is working for the devil and really does not care for the sheep. What he is seeking is "divinity for himself as well as for his Master, Sanat Kamura, aka. fallen Lucifier. The means are trickery and deceit. Such guile tarnishes and defiles all pure motives.

When Pam looks back over 31 years, even though she was snatched so quickly and utterly from Maitreya's hands into the kingdom of Jesus Christ, Maitreya was certainly "not through with her!!!!" The trap for her as a Christian was set even though she was born again. What our founder has learned by experience is that when demons lose their hold on a captive, they usually try to leave "a calling card" behind---an emblem of sorts that sends the message, "you STILL belong to me.!!!" For example, they will use people to place demonic objects strategically in your house or car.

In Pam's case, Maitreya decided to "sneak his calling card" into her ministerial hand by secretly suggesting that she call her ministry "healing waters." Maitreya reasoned, "when Pam gives her testimony of how she was rescued from the occult, people who know about me will believe that she is still affiliated with "new age" because of her ministerial name and fearful Christians will "stay away from her" or "not take her seriously." Even so, Pam sees things rather clearly now that she knows that "healing waters" is a Maitreya expression, symbolizing his so-called healing ability to perform counterfeit miracles where natural bodies of water are apparently energized to produce "a healing".

So from personal experience, Pam is wise enough to know that God will stay His Hand, according to His own purpose. When we wonder why God does not act against the holocaust of human history, a very simple answer evades us so we say that He is either non-existent, not powerful, or if He exists, He does not care and we ball up our fists, and wave them angrily toward heaven. Yet the cross, the sacrifice of Jesus at Calvary contradicts us, for God DOES care because He gave His only begotten Son to become sin on our behalf. So anyone with good, logical sense should come to the conclusion that "there MUST be another answer." Here is the clue to solving the mystery of Maitreya. What does Maitreya and man have in common?

From the garden, we have been at enmity with the devil and his demonic troops, yet we have one thing in common. Both the fallen and man believe that we can succeed in saving this planet. Whether united or divided, both man and the devil desire to boast, "we are the savior." As such, our faith in ourselves reveals that we are NOT dependent upon God. Since we have demonstrated our capacity and our skills, and some of us even boast that "we are anointed" -- we even fool ourselves into believing that we can establish our own kingdoms on earth, either for ourselves or on God's behalf. This message has also infiltrated the organized church with the false doctrine of motivational speakers who pass themselves off as tv evangelists. In addition, the organized church has been preaching that man himself can choose the time and season of his own salvation.

Without a doubt, the climax of the events about to take place on planet earth, suggests that God's plans require complete, unconditional surrender from EVERYBODY!!!. Both man and the anti-Christ shall have to come face to face with their mutual spiritual depravity and surrender to the fact that the Father's only answer for the late, great planet earth is the return of the Lord Jesus Christ of Nazareth. Every knee shall bow and every tongue shall confess that **Jesus Christ is LORD!!!!**

CHAPTER SEVEN

Church Can Be Dangerous!

The plan for Maitreya's entrance into the earth's sphere in recent times was established through the Jezebel spirit of two previously mentioned women: Helen Blavatsky in 1875 and Alice Bailey from 1919-1949. Both of these women claimed to have received their information telepathically from one or more of the ascended masters and both of these women had strong ties to the organized church. Called the Mother of the New Age Movement, Alice Bailey was originally a member of the Presbyterian church. However, It could be that when Jesus referred to "that woman Jezebel," it is quite possible that he was actually referring to the deification of His own mother as an ascended master who is worshiped by both Roman Catholics, various Christian cults and new age occultists as "Mother Mary."

MOTHER MARY

While Catholics believe they are appropriately venerating the Virgin Mary and Divine Child Jesus within the parameters of Biblical tradition, the evidence is overwhelming that Roman Catholics have been deceived into fostering and continuing the Egyptian and Babylonian pagan tradition of worshiping the Sun Goddess Isis and her Divine Son. It is obvious to the discerning that the deification of Mary is a natural by-product of ancient old world cults. In Christiandom, the counterfeit Mary has certainly assumed the functions of ancient pagan goddesses as it relates to motherhood, procreation and sex. Members of Christian cults, Roman Catholics and the new age movement have different beliefs relative to whom they call Mother Mary. What should be emphasized here is that "Mother Mary" is not the Lord's real mother but a masquerading demon.

Within Christian cults like Mormonism, though well hidden today among the church of the Latter Day Saints, the first Mormons blasphemously taught that the Father actually had sex with Mary to conceive His Son.

> "The fleshly body of Jesus required a Mother as well as a Father. Therefore, the Father and Mother of Jesus, according to the flesh, must have been associated in the capacity of husband and wife; hence the Virgin Mary must have been, for the time being, the lawful wife of God the Father: we use the term lawful wife, because it would be blasphemous in the highest degree to say that He overshadowed her or begat the Savior unlawfully........He had a lawful right to overshadow the Virgin Mary IN THE CAPACITY OF A HUSBAND, and beget a Son.......Whether God the Father gave Mary to Joseph for time only, or for time and eternity, we are not informed. It may be that He only gave her to be the wife of Joseph while in this mortal state, and that He intended after the resurrection to again take her as one of his own wives to raise up immortal spirits in eternity." Apostle Orson Pratt, "The Seer," Oct. 1853, p. 158).

To counter any repugnance from its followers concerning how God actually had sexual intercourse with the human Mary, Apostle Pratt employed some "spiritual babble" by teaching that Mary was one of God's polygamous "celestial wives." However, the founding fathers and leaders of the Church of Jesus Christ of Latter-Day Saints proclaimed that Jesus Christ is the Son of God in THE MOST LITERAL SENSE. The body in which Jesus Christ of Nazareth performed His mission in the flesh was believed by founders and leaders of Mormonism to be SIRED by that same God whom we worship as God, our Eternal Father." Found among the writings of early Mormonism are articles that reflect Mormon understanding that God actually had sex with Mary, a belief that uphold's Mary's divinity for she was not spiritually married to Joseph but to God the Father.

Yet another so-called "Christian" cult like Moonie's Unification Church is even more perverse on this subject than the Mormons. They teach that Mary had sex with Zechariah, John the Baptist's father, and that Jesus was their illegitimate son, the half brother of John the Baptist. It is painful to even write such a thing, but you need to know the impact of such teachings upon those who seek Jesus. They end up duped into worshiping "the Fake Jesus."

People who have worshiped under the authority of churches that spread perverse teachings have suffered from all kinds of demonic torment, particularly sexual perversions of all kinds, including homosexuality, incest, pedophilia, bestiality and masturbation. Through experiential learning, we have noticed a particular trend among Catholic men who are enslaved to pornography and sexual addictions of all kinds. Today we have a better sense of the cause of this spiritual phenomena and we have revisede the deliverance counseling intervention, as needed.

While Roman Catholics believe they are venerating the Virgin Mary and Divine Child Jesus within a legitimate, scriptural tradition, the evidence is overwhelming that they are really continuing the Egyptian and Babylonian pagan tradition of worshiping the Sun Goddess Isis and her Divine Son. We first began to have suspicions that the church at Thyatira might be connected to Roman Catholicism when we read in the news about a strange event that took place in Naples over 5 years ago.

As predominately Roman Catholic children were celebrating Halloween in a school house in Naples, the ground opened with a devastating earthquake, and 25 children were buried alive under a mass of broken buildings and cement. The fact that Roman Catholics profess to be Christian yet they were allowing their children to celebrate the devil's day is a story unto itself. However, within our own scriptural view of the events, we reflected upon Revelation, the 3rd Chapter. Our understanding is based upon one key hypothesis. We had suspected that the Roman Catholic church is the modern day church at Thyatira---a church that Jesus both commended and rebuked. He praised the church at Thyatira because of her works of service to humanity. It is a well known fact that there is no church on earth that can compare to the compassionate endeavors of the Roman Catholic church around the world for needy and oppressed people.

However, the Lord Jesus Christ also rebuked the Thyatiran church because of a woman that Jesus referred to as Jezebel. In Rev. Ch. 3, the following words of the Lord to this church are recorded: "You tolerate that woman Jezebel, who calls herself a prophetess. By her teaching she misleads my servants into fornication and the eating of food sacrificed to idols. I have given her time to repent of her immorality, but she is unwilling. I will cast her on a bed of suffering, and I will make those who commit adultery with her suffer intensely, unless they repent of her ways. "

Notwithstanding, it is the following verse that we believe has begun to be fulfilled in our times, as seen in Naples on 10/31/02. "I will strike her children DEAD. Then all the churches shall know that I am He who searches hearts and minds, and I will repay each of you according to your deeds." Prior to the earthquake in Naples , we took this statement metaphorically, believing that this verse did not necessarily refer to actual deaths. Perhaps the sexual molestation of countless Roman Catholic children over the years by priests is yet another sign of the fulfillment of this particular verse. However, unfortunately, when we viewed a TV News show and observed a brief shot of the Pope's grief stricken face, our hearts felt heavy.

Certainly church can be confusing since there are so many of them. Simply put, there are two main sects of Christians: Catholics and

Protestants. Within Protestantism, there are three main branches: the denominations, the non-denominations, and the word of faith/charismatic movement. There are many denominations. A few denominations are charismatic, ie. the pentecostal churches. There is one denomination that calls itself "full gospel baptist." It should be pointed out that every non-denominational church is not necessarily charismatic or word of faith. However, practically ALL word of faith churches are charismatic and therefore they have much in common with some denominational pentecostal churches.

CATHOLICISM

Over centuries of time, there is no doubt that Roman Catholicism has created "a Jezebel" out of the Lord's mother Mary. Defined within this context, a "Jezebel" is a false prophetess or a religious goddess. For example, it is true that Mary was a virgin when Jesus was conceived but she did not remain a virgin when she became the mother of James and the Lord's other brothers and sisters. Incredibly, the Roman Catholic Church has gone so far as to declare that Mary herself was conceived immaculately. Yet, in scripture, one could surmise that there was some friction between Jesus and His family during the course of His three year ministry.

This is why when Mary and the Lord's siblings sought to speak with Him, Jesus was less than responsive when told that his family was waiting outside. In fact, He practically retorted when He retorted, "my mother and my brothers are those who hear the word of God and obey it." In other words, the implication was that His natural family was not obeying the word of God, and that might also have included Mary. Mary was at the cross, and John took care of her for her remaining years. She was a saint in the same way that all who follow the Lord Jesus Christ are called "saints." That means you, if you are born again. In short, Mary is dead, her spirit is with God but her body is in the grave as others who have died or will die in Jesus.

In the Bible, the words fornication and idolatry were connected. In heathen nations like Ephesus for example, prostitutes would have sex with men right in the temple to appease the goddess Diana. Throughout the old testament, God would speak to His people through the prophets and call them harlots because they followed after or worshiped other gods of neighboring heathen nations. Could it be that the Lord is saying to the church at Thyatira, "you have created a goddess out of a woman to worship her?" In this way this particular church age may have committed fornication and idolatry and have broken His commandment which says that we shall have no other gods but Him!"

The Lord Jesus Christ is merciful and full of grace. For centuries, He has tolerated this competition with the false image the Roman Catholic Church has created of His birth mother. In his internet article entitled "The Truth About Roman Catholicism" by M.H. Reynolds, you will find these words

> "The place accorded Mary in the Roman Catholic Church is not scriptural nor is it new, but it cannot be denied that, during the last one hundred years, veneration of Mary has dramatically increased....note that the exaltation of Mary and the term, Mother of God, became official Catholic dogma in 431 AD with prayers to her proclaimed in 600 A.D. But, note also that the Immaculate Conception of the Virgin Mary was not proclaimed until 1854; her 'Assumption' not until 1950; and her title 'Mother of the Church"'not until as recently as 1965."

http://catholic.cephasministry.com/the_truth_about_catholicism.html

The major confusion is centered in the scriptural understanding of Mary's virginity. Yet, all women are born virgins "until they have sex." This does not make them "divine" for we are all sinners, virgin or not. However, Christians who deify her, reason that since Jesus is the creative principle within the trinity of the godhead. Therefore, it is believed that Mary is herself divine because she bore the Creator of the world."

Furthermore, Mary is also viewed as "the cause of redemption." So, we believe that the His mother's deification is extremely upsetting to Jesus. In fact, the Lord clearly taught that in heaven, sexual distinction does not exist. Jesus has given Jezebel time to repent. A word of comfort to those born Roman Catholic who have become "born again." Jesus said to the church at Thyatira, "Now I say to the rest of you in Thyatira, to you who do not hold to her teaching, and have not learned Satan's so-called deep secrets, I will not impose any other burden on you. Only hold on to what you have until I come."(Rev 3:24,25)

Occultists and new agers believe that Mother Mary is an ascended master, a human being who has become divine because she gave birth to the reincarnated Jesus Sananda and she herself was the reincarnation of several other women. Occultist claim that ascended master Mary, the mother of the Lord Jesus, is one of the 'Ascended Masters' who channels messages of peace on an ever increasing magnitude.

As we have studied some of the channeled rhetoric about "Mother Mary," it seems that her focus is signs, wonders, healing and miracles. Perhaps we can now understand the significance of the many apparitions -- so beloved by Roman Catholics -- of the Virgin Mary throughout the present century, in which she calls repeatedly for the setting-up of a global brotherhood to usher in an earthly reign of peace and justice. The pictorial form in which this Ascended Master Mother Mary, is represented in the occult literature is virtually identical to the form of the Virgin Mary which appears in Roman Catholic visions and apparitions. Mother Mary is the 'Archetypal "Mother God"', and it is difficult to avoid the conclusion that for centuries Roman Catholics have been hoodwinked into regarding a demonic discarnate deception as a genuine vision of the mother of Jesus Christ. In other words, the Virgin Mary of the visions is an evil spirit.

One of the most renowned of more recent apparitions is that which frequently appears in Medjugorje in Bosnia. As a fallen angel,------ the demon called Mother Mary has been drawing countless numbers of international travelers to the village, where a select group of young men and women have ecstatic visions and report their communications to the eagerly awaiting folk in attendance. This demon has reportedly given the youngsters ten prophetic secrets to be revealed before their occurrence in order to convince the world of their authenticity. In common with the other 'Ascended Masters', this demonic apparition preaches 'Peace, peace, when there is no peace' (Jer.6:14). One occult group characterizes this particular fallen angel as communicating such messages as:

'I am not only your mother but your very personal friend. I ask you to take my hand, to take me to your home, to accept me as your friend'. In Medjugorje, she transmits lengthy messages which are repeatedly punctuated with the eerie, robotic phrase: 'Thank you for responding to my call...thank you for responding to my call...thank you for responding to my call, etc'. (Taken from http://richardboyden.com/ascended_masters.htm)

As with every other ascended master, the rhetoric concerning them is prolific, conflicting and confusing. Therefore, our research targets what we perceive to be the underlying motive of the demon. Concerning the demon called "Mother Mary," in a quotation taken directly from occult writings is the underlying blasphemy that is akin to Jezebel:

> **Jesus didn't come to save us;**
> he came to show us how to save ourselves by changing our consciousness. And Mother Mary gives us another very,very important example of that.

This sole statement is the key. Saved by works is the underlying error of both Catholicism, Christian cults and new age occultism---in other words, THAT WE CAN SAVE OURSELVES. Ascended master literature is so extensive that it is nearly unmanageable. As a sample of it, we have included below a bit of channeled verbiage of the demon who calls itself "Mother Mary." You will observe that the underlying message is yet the same: THAT WE CAN SAVE OURSELVES, WITHOUT A NEED FOR THE CROSS!. According to Mother Mary, "ALL WE NEED TO DO IS TO COMMUNICATE WITH OUR "CHAIN OF BEING." THE CHAIN OF BEING INCLUDES THE ASCENDED MASTERS. READ THE FOLLOWING WORDS CHANNELLED BY THE DEMON aka ascended master "MOTHER MARY:"

> "The reason why people on Earth are not guaranteed to be saved is that most of them have become trapped in the consciousness of duality in which they see themselves separated from their source. Ultimately, your source is God, but because you are an extension of the Chain of Being that reaches from the Creator to you, your source really is the entire chain of being, meaning all spiritual

beings above you. Thus, the ONLY road to salvation or immortality is to attain oneness with your entire Chain of Being. People need to be saved because they have become separated from their source, so the only road to salvation is to overcome this separation. And when you do so, you will not only see yourself as one with God but as one with the entire spiritual hierarchy above you.

As I said, your conscious self is an extension of the Creator's Being and thus you can experience the Creator directly. This experience really does happen through the Chain of Being above you, but an immature seeker may not be aware of this. Likewise, any communication from God to you happens through the Chain of Being, and again an immature seeker may not be aware of this. So it is possible that people will receive communication from above without realizing that it comes through the Chain of Being which is the same as the ascended masters or the Ascended Host.

Mary, Mother of Jesus, is also known as Lady Master of Comfort and Nurturing. Within the charismatic church is an emphasis on inner healing, an ascended master influence associated with this particular fallen angel. Mother Mary's responsibilities include teaching her followers to accept and express hurtful and darker feelings as a part of their emotional healing. Mother Mary also claims to oversee the imbalance of what is called "mother/feminine energies, lunacy, madness and violence---in other words, as an ascended master, Mother Mary is supposed to hinder earth's catastrophes and chaos. In the reverse, anyone who prays to Mother Mary with rosaries, burns candles to her and the like, are putting themselves "in harms way."

As previously mentioned, another major duty is to bring about unity through a one world religion. As the Mother of God, the Fake Mary lifts up the mission of her son, the Fake Jesus. Typically, there is an obvious rivalry between ascended master Jesus Sananda and Mother Mary. How can Mary be called and accepted as the Mother of God by occultists and new agers who do not themselves believe that her son Jesus Himself IS GOD! So in a confusing, conflicting way in New Age beliefs, Mother Mary surpasses Jesus Sananda in power and influence.

As would be expected, new agers believe that Mother Mary was also a part of the human chain of reincarnation. For example, occultists teach that prior to her incarnation as Mary, in another life, Mary served in the healing temples of Atlantis. Occultist claim Mary was also the mother of King David,--that King David who was an incarnation of Jesus Sananda, making Mary the mother of both the Jewish and Christian faiths. Mary's husband, Joseph, guardian of Jesus, is claimed to be the reincarnation of a familiar fallen angel, St.Germain.

The apparition that imitates Mother Mary has appeared to people on Earth several times at Lourdes and Fatima, and many miracles are attributed to her from these visitations. She asks us to pray to her using the rosary. Mother Mary is further known as the Queen of the Angels and her followers claim that she works constantly with them on the ray of compassion. She is the ascended master whose primary responsibility is to protect women and children and Mary is said to be a healer. The occultists make no bones about it, claiming that Mother Mary is the reincarnation of Isis, when she instructed initiates in the Mystery Schools. Those who have blasphemed the true Jesus with their worship of His mother have been given time to repent. How much time were they given? We believe several centuries. What does this group have that he or she can hold on to? Well, the word "catholic" without the influence of Rome means "universal."

As such, all who believe on Jesus Christ are "catholic," as is stated in various affirmations of faith recited in most churches. Church members declare that they believe in the "HOLY" catholic church, not the "Roman." If you read the Bible for yourself and examine with a rational mind the doctrines of your faith according to it, a Roman Catholic will come to know that no one should pray to Mary or to any other saint.

If a professing Roman Catholic does not pray with rosaries, nor eat bread and wine that has unknowingly been sacrificed to demons, if a Roman Catholic realizes that there is no such place as purgatory, and stops calling a man 'Father', does not participate in Mass, and accepts the fact that his or her good works are commendable, but they will not get anyone into heaven. If the Holy Ghost leads a Roman Catholic to repent and gives him or her a measure of faith to believe that Jesus Christ of Nazareth was raised from the dead by the Holy Spirit, then a Roman Catholic can be saved and burden free! The irony is that all of these beliefs and practices are what distinguishes a Roman Catholic from every other born again Christian. I ponder on the question, "What if the time the Lord has given the church at Thyatira to repent has now passed and that committed Roman Catholics are today "out of time?" We wonder.

In a nutshell, the body of the real Mary, Mother of God is in the grave. At her death like any other Christian, to be absent from the body is to be present with the Lord. So Mary is clearly in heaven with the rest of the departed saints, waiting upon her Son to return to earth and raise her ashes from out of her burial tomb. Yet, there is another "Mary in the heavens" and it is not the Lord's mother. This fallen angel resides in the heavens that surround earth and NOT in third heaven where Jesus is at the right hand of His Father. Rather, in accord with Roman Catholics and occultist new agers who venerate the biblical Mary as an ascended master along with Maitreya, Sananda, Germaine and a host of other fallen angels, there is a cosmic demon that is also called "Mother Mary."

If the admiration of Mary becomes anything more than using her as a model of faith in God the Father, those who have deified her delve into dangerous spiritual territory. They are actually worshiping a demon. Elevating either the Lord's real mother or the demon to a position of divine status is alarming. Mary can be a Christian role model (like Paul or Peter, Sarah, or Ruth) for our faith, but she is not divine nor is she able to provide for our salvation. Jesus Christ alone is God and is the only person capable of enabling the salvation of all mankind. The Word of God is explicit on this subject.

The Ascended Master "Mother" Mary is an obvious counterfeit, for no where in the bible are there any female angels. Therefore, this effeminate demonic impostor who pretends to be the mother of the Messiah is a masculine demon in drag---a gay demon, if you will. In keeping with the sexual distortions surrounding the fake Mary, it becomes more understandable as to the reason that so many Catholic men in general and priest in particular are perverse in their sexuality---several of whom have contacted us for counseling. The sad testimony of the following Roman Catholic man is a classic example, endemic of what devotion to the "goddess" Mary can do to a man's sexuality:

> Ever since middle school I was called fag because I never had a girlfriend or never was having sex. I choose to be a virgin until marriage. It wasn't until I was 13 until I realized I was turned on by gay pornography. Masturbation was very common. and when i went to college I had oral sex with a guy like 8 times. I feel horrible and I still look at gay pornography but I like women even though I haven't been in a relationship. I'm not confused as I have debated with myself several times.

I need forgiveness and help. I know some may identify

me as a bi sexual but I don't want that. I know my lust may be a result of being a virgin. I hate that I have done these things. It kills me inside but if I can overcome, it almost consumes most of my life. there are many things that I need to pray about but this being number one problem. Women and men are attractive to me even though I would only feel comfortable with a woman.

Over the last 5 years, several men have contacted us either for prayer or for deliverance counseling with the exact same problem. In fact, most of them could have written this testimony themselves. Recently, we heard a despicable account of how a young boy picked up a demon while actually in a Catholic classroom. It seems the teacher purposefully sat with her legs wide open so that she could catch any of the boys trying to look up her dress. When this particular boy was caught, she kept him after class. She made him pull down his pants and she beat him with a belt on his backside until he ejaculated. Since that day, this boy, now an adult, has a spirit of sexual perversion, manifested in an out of control cycle of voyeurism, pornography, masturbation, cross dressing, and masochism.

Without the sexual component, the definition of masochism has a very Roman Catholic sound to it--1. The deriving of sexual gratification, or the tendency to derive sexual gratification, from being physically or emotionally abused. 2. The deriving of pleasure, or the tendency to derive pleasure, from being humiliated or mistreated, either by another or by oneself. 3. A willingness or tendency to subject oneself to unpleasant or trying experiences. When you consider the generic definition of the Roman Catholic doctrine of "penance", -an act of self-mortification or devotion performed voluntarily to show sorrow for a sin or other wrongdoing--there is an eerie similarity between masochism and penance.

Unfortunately, we have not had one successful deliverance with Roman Catholic men primarily because they will only commit themselves to one, no more than two consultations. As such, it extremely difficult to convince this group of male captives to enroll in counseling for any length of time, primarily because captives to sexual perversion derive a subliminal or even conscious pleasure from being humiliated or mistreated. We suspect that this is the work of the fallen angel, the ascended master who calls itself "Mother Mary." Its influence around the world both in Roman Catholicism, Christian cults, occultism, sexual perversion and gender confusion is beyond our estimation. The numbers of those affected by "Mother Mary" is staggering, perhaps surpassing both Maitreya., Germaine and even Sananda.

PROTESTANTISM

Our suspicion that the age of the organized church is either over or very close to ending has been growing over time. One crucial, yet potentially damnable sign of the end of the gentile age is mounting evidence that souls are not being saved in the organized church. What is really troublesome is that we are finding that even the best churches can be hazardous, primarily because subtle deception is actually held in place by the sincerity and the commitment of its leadership. To be sincerely wrong can be almost as deadly as being obviously deceived or purposefully deceptive. From our own vantage point from a deliverance perspective, we have been put in contact with demonized churchgoers around the country and even the world. As such, there is one major sign that suggests that the church age may be coming to a close. We are willing to bet that some of you are guessing that the most outstanding sign of the demise of the Protestant church is either dying churches, sinning preachers, the prosperity gospel or even false prophets. These are certainly signs that "Satan has a seat". But the most outstanding sign is that Satan may be standing behind the pulpit because one of his cosmic beings, Sananda, has paved the way for him.

Consider this. The main reason why the church was commissioned in the first place was to preach a gospel that the Holy Spirit could use to draw the elect to the cross of Jesus Christ of Nazareth. Yet for 200 years or more, the gospel has been tainted with an insidious error that no one seems to be able to correct and most ministers are totally unaware of it. In a nutshell, the main error is that the people are being taught worldwide that "God will save them once they make a decision to choose Jesus Christ of Nazareth.---that the ability to be saved lies in man's hands."

Such a teaching borders on blasphemy because if man is saved by "accepting Jesus," then the decision is a work of man and not a gift from God according to grace, "lest any man should boast and declare "I am saved because I ACCEPTED JESUS! Whether denominational or non-denominational, pentecostal or Charismatic, practically the entire Protestant church upholds the "free will" decision approach to salvation. Do you yourself believe that you can or could be saved anytime that YOU wanted to? Do you believe that you are NOW saved simply because you responded to an altar call and/ or you repeated a sinner's prayer where you "asked Jesus to come into your heart?" If you can answer in the affirmative, then you have been deceived and therein, defiled! You are in jeopardy on judgment day when the Lord looks at you and declares,"I NEVER KNEW YOU!!"

Alarmingly, what is being preached in practically ALL of the Protestant churches is that through a personal decision--the volition and choice of human will---the lost can ACCEPT Christ to be saved. This is a tenet that has so strongly grieved the Holy Ghost, that it is reasonable to wonder if He has left Protestantism entirely. As previously mentioned, started by a preacher called Charles Finney about 200 years ago, this foundational error has pervasively spread like yeast throughout every corner of the Protestant church. Even the most renowned evangelist of our time, Billy Graham has also preached the " make a decision" doctrine of salvation to millions upon millions.

Moreover, the church practice of the invitation to Christian discipleship through an altar call and the repeating of "the sinner's prayer" are the main anchors that hold the foundation of the "free will method" in place in its attempt to convince the lost that they must be saved by "choosing Christ" before it is too late. Some will even preach the doctrine of hell as a scare tactic to browbeat a "decision for Christ." The essential root of the problem is that when a person sits in church, in a huge stadium, watches a TV evangelist, or even "is led to Christ" by another professing Christian, the lost are being taught that they can ACCEPT Jesus into their own hearts and salvation is automatically theirs for the asking.

Interestingly enough, no where in the word of God is it written that "we accept Christ into our hearts." Paul wrote to the Romans that we "believe in our hearts that Christ was raised from the dead." However, Paul did not write that we must "accept Jesus into our hearts." When we are born again, Jesus does not "enter our hearts." How can He enter our hearts when He is at the right hand of the Father??? This is why the Lord told His disciples that it was better for them that He go away so that the Holy Ghost would come. The Holy Ghost is that part of the godhead who enters our spirits, causing us to become "temples of God." The heart and the spirit are two distinctively different entities in man. Similarly, like the words "rapture" and "purgatory",the phrase "accept Jesus" is yet another religious euphemism, not backed up by scripture.

Furthermore, the message of "I accepted Christ" is so preposterous that it is an offense to the triune Godhead. We DO NOT ACCEPT CHRIST. NO ONE CAN BE SAVED UNLESS GOD HIMSELF HAS ALREADY MADE THE CHOICE!!!! The Father and the Son have already done the choosing or the electing before the beginning of recorded time. When the sinner actually hears the call, he simply responds. Even when a sinner cries out for Jesus, it may appear to be an act of his own free will, yet the Lord said that no man can come to Him unless the Father which sent Him draws them. (John 6:44)

Subsequently, even when a sinner begs the Lord for mercy to save him, he does so because he has been drawn to the cross by the Holy Ghost. Therefore, even our repentance is not human but godly. Godly sorrow is a repentance for sin that has been divinely given to the sinner to cause him to repent, to sorrow over the Lord's sacrifice. At the cross, a sinner's spirit is washed, cleansed and forgiven by the blood of Jesus Christ of Nazareth.

It is important to state here that nothing stops God, not even the church. When the Lord is ready for the elect, He calls them. If they are sitting on a church pew, He can still reach them, regardless of what they have been listening to. The problem is that many of the elect who are in church believe that they are already saved but they are not. The Father plans to save them. Nevertheless, for the Holy Ghost to draw them to a genuine salvation experience, the strong man must be bound with the light of truth. In this instance, the "strong man" is the religious demon, aka,the Fake Jesus.

In the beginning of our work in deliverance counseling , we were shocked and horrified at the manifestations that emanated from professing Christians. To hear even tongue talkers be used by demons to roar, growl and shout blasphemies that include 4 letter words is so astounding, that it an can be rather disconcerting, to say the least. What we have found is that religious demons are now dwelling in the human spirit of professing Christians, the place which is intended for the Holy Ghost. We have also learned that these demons must be cast out first, before the Holy Ghost will enter.

This is a formidable task because religiosity has become "a high tower"in the lives of the lost who insist that they are saved. This high tower must be pulled down by truth, brick by brick. Simply put, attempting to reach a churchgoer who believes that he is saved because he repeated a sinner's prayer and accepted Jesus "into his heart" is like trying to put a camel through the eye of a needle. But as the Lord declared, "what is impossible for men is possible with God."I marvel at what the Lord is doing.

Grieved and quenched, it has been our experience that the Holy Ghost will not move either the called or the chosen by the "free will" method because the gospel has not been properly preached. Since faith comes by hearing the gospel, we need to understand "what the gospel is." The gospel is plain and simple yet very rarely heard in what is commonly known as "a sermon." In fact, most sermons heard in churches today are "not the gospel of Jesus Christ." They may be interesting, inspiring, enthusiastic, joyous, dramatic, charismatic and even life changing relative to coping with the natural challenges and circumstances of life. Yet, unless the gospel of the kingdom is preached in every sermon, the Holy Ghost will not draw anyone to the cross and without the cross, no one will be saved. You may cry, shout, jump up and even fall on your face yet without the complete truth, there will be no fruit that leads to eternal life.

In truth, Protestant preachers of all persuasions have been using sermons to convict and to convince, sometimes through coercion. As such, some have attempted to do a job that is only meant for the Holy Ghost. No, our job is simple. We are merely to "tell the story" and the Holy Ghost uses our "story telling" of the gospel by convicting and convincing the lost Himself. Essential to the story we tell,---whether it be in a sermon, a conversation, a letter, or a personal testimony---we must "preach the gospel of Jesus Christ." Certainly, the gospel of Jesus Christ is routinely repeated on Sundays within various denominational affirmations of faith: Jesus was born, crucified,buried,rose to life in His own physical body on the third day, ascended and He's coming back. In a nutshell, THIS IS THE GOSPEL---plain and simple. Yet preachers never seem to run out of subjects for a Sunday morning sermon. For example, if they preach about faith, ---what it is, what it does, how to get it,---unless the message on faith is directly connected to His crucifixion, His resurrection, His ascension and His return, the Holy Ghost will not use a great "faith" sermon to save not one soul. Even though hell is real, a sermon that tries to coerce a commitment to Christ out of a fear of going to hell will not bare fruit either.

So what are the essential ingredients to a bonafide conversion? Well, a crucial aspect of the gospel is that we are all dead in our trespasses and sins. So I ask you, "How can a dead man save himself?" He can't. A dead man needs to be resurrected. As Jesus raised Lazarus from the dead in the natural, He did not raise Himself from the dead because "He was dead." The bible tells us that Jesus was raised by the glory of the Father. In another scripture it reads that Jesus was raised by the power of the Holy Ghost. Therefore, it logically follows that "the glory of the Father is the Holy Ghost. If a equals b and c equals b, then a also equals c. Simple.

As Jesus raised Lazarus from the dead in the natural, and as the Holy Ghost raised Jesus from the dead in the natural, we cannot raise ourselves from the dead in spirit by making a "decision" or by repeating words. How does a dead man in the natural make a decision when he can't even blink an eyelash? Dead is dead. Death cannot raise itself to life. No, only the Holy Ghost can raise US from being dead in the spirit to eternal life. Jesus said that the Holy Ghost would save us "like the wind." When the wind blows, it takes us by surprise. Then we see the results of the wind by what has been left behind. When the Holy Ghost blows, someone is going to be "born again." (John 3) The sign that the Holy Ghost may have left the organized church is that "the wind is not blowing there." When we confess the Lord Jesus with our mouths, the wind has "already blown"on us and we have already been "raised from the dead" in the spirit. Repeated in another way, when we confess that we believe that Jesus was raised from the dead, the Holy Ghost has already given us a measure of faith to believe that a dead man lives again. Moreover,Jesus said that no man can come to Him unless the Father Who sent Him draws them. The Father draws the elect to Christ by the Holy Ghost. Repentance, conviction of sin, coming to the cross and believing on the resurrection is the sole work of the Holy Ghost as He translates the dead in sin into newness of eternal life.

Therefore, the Holy Ghost does the entire job of calling the lost whom God has chosen from the beginning of time to be His elect. All we are required to do is PREACH THE GOSPEL OF JESUS CHRIST! WE DON'T LEAD ANYONE TO CHRIST. The fact that the organized church has stood in the place of the Holy Ghost, attempted to do what only He can do, is a sign that the Holy Ghost is NOT pleased. Has He been blasphemed? I tremble at the thought. When He is blasphemed, then we will see with our own eyes, yet another sign, the Abomination of Desolation.

So think about it. When have you really heard the gospel preached?--- Jesus Christ as crucified, dead, buried, resurrected, ascended and "comin back." Most people who are sitting on a pew every week do not even understand the bodily resurrection of the Lord Jesus Christ, as they believe that He was raised merely as a spirit, in spite of the fact that the scriptures tell us that after Jesus was raised, He cooked, He ate and He told Thomas to touch Him, just to prove to the doubter that He was alive in His flesh and bone body.

The confusion comes in the interpretation of a verse in the 15th chapter of First Corinthians where Paul referred to being raised "a spiritual" body. Paul did not intend to suggest that Jesus was raised as a spirit only. No, a spiritual body is actually a physical body that has been glorified. A glorified or "spiritual body" is not a spirit alone without substance. A glorified body is a material, physical body that have been changed to immortality, incapable of dying A PHYSICAL DEATH AGAIN. Once again, a spiritual body is not "a spirit" or a ghost.

As uniformly is the case, the lack of understanding of the resurrection among both traditional and particularly charismatic church goers is a sign that the church has failed primarily because of the lack of preaching and teaching concerning the bodily resurrection of the Lord Jesus Christ of Nazareth. Pastors world wide assume that all of their members understand the resurrection. And as quiet as its kept, there are untold preachers who don't understand the resurrection either. As is the crucifixion, the resurrection is paramount to salvation. Paul told the Corinthians that if they did not believe on the bodily resurrection of the Lord Jesus Christ, their faith was vain. Not only that but Paul warned, "you are STILL in your sins." In other words, if you don't believe on the resurrection in the correct way, you are NOT SAVED. (I Corinthians 15:17)

We use a simple screening test that in deliverance counseling wherein we ask the client to explain the resurrection. If they are unable to explain the expression "He rose from the dead," then they are obviously NOT saved. So ask yourself from your own experience, "Is the gospel being preached on Sunday mornings?" Rarely, during the Lenten season and rarely on Easter Sunday, and thats IT!!!

In order for people to be saved, they need to hear messages that focus on sin, being lost, repentance, the cross, the blood, the resurrection, and the Lord's return. This is the gospel, plain and simple. The Holy Ghost has been grieved a long time because He cannot use faulty preaching in either a lofty, scholarly exhortation or a down home "earthy" sermon to draw anyone to Jesus Christ. In a nutshell, with what is being preached from the pulpits on a Sunday morning, there is insufficient saving power in the typical sermon. The Holy Ghost will not draw anyone to Christ with what is being preached. So we believe that this circumstance is a significant sign that He may have already left the premises. Ichabod!

Sinning preachers can repent. False prophets can be exposed. False doctrine can be corrected. But how does the organized church fix an error that is actually built into the language of the system, words that are heard coming from the mouths of practically EVERY professing Christian who proudly boasts, "I accepted Christ." It bares repeating. No one accepts Christ to be saved. He has already accepted us from the beginning of time and not the other way around. When every one of the elect is saved, the world as we know it "will be toast." Why? Because the true Jesus will return and literally TAKE OVER!!!!

So consider this. If our salvation was anchored solely in a decision of our willpower, wouldn't salvation be obtained by the works of our own flesh and not by the grace of God? **We would be able to boast, "I made the decision to accept Jesus Christ."** It bares repeating once again that the elect were chosen in Jesus Christ before Adam and Eve were even created. We cannot even repent to be saved without the help of the Holy Ghost. The faith to believe on Jesus Christ is not even ours. The Holy Ghost even gives us the faith to believe on the Lord's resurrection. When we confess that Jesus is Lord, we have already been saved.

We could back up these words with many scriptures. Even though the word of God suggests that the organized church will continue to exist and operate until the Lord's return, we suspect that few souls will be saved at its altars because of the Holy Ghost may have already vacated the sanctuary, that the fake Jesus is almost totally in control, and the organized church may have recently been judged or will be judged very soon. Once the Holy Ghost has left the organized church, then local churches and denominations will become increasingly defiled and eventually, fully apostate, as it transforms into the Harlot.

In truth, we hope that we are wrong. However, one man, **Charles Finney**, has led to the greatest falling away that probably Paul himself did not even imagine would transpire. So if souls are not being saved in either the Catholic or the Protestant churches, then the organized church has lost its usefulness. The "make a decision, I accepted Jesus gospel is so permeated within church tradition, that it seems that the organized church is incapable of fixing a problem that has been built deep into its foundation for about 200 years. In fact, most of the church is not even aware of this essential problem. So the enemy has had his seat in it for quite some time. The scriptures point to a Satanic "take over" of the organized church through the clever work of one of his best soldiers, the religious demon, the spirit of the Anti-Christ aka, Jesus Sananda Immanuel, aka "The Fake Jesus.". When this occurs, we will experience "the abomination of desolation" and we must stand in the holy place. Where is the holy place? Is the holy place in Jerusalem, the Rock of the Dome as some endtime specialists contend? If so, how could we "stand in the holy place?" Are there enough planes to fly every Christian to Jerusalem or money to pay the price for mass travel?

So where is "the holy place?" Well we suggest to you that it is wherever you can find the Holy Ghost!!!! If our suspicions are correct and the Holy Ghost has already moved out of the church, then He is saving folk outside of church walls. He has certainly not stopped His work---He has merely changed His location. The Holy Ghost is falling on people in the streets, at home, on the job, at the club, on the bus, you name it, He's there. And the lost will find themselves at the feet of the cross and not be able to even explain "how they got there!"

One clear, illustrative sign out of several such cases is a recent testimony from a woman who sat in a Baptist church for more than 20 years, going through the circle of falling away and rededicating herself to Christ, over and over again.--baptized more than once. She herself admitted that in 20 years of church attendance, she now realizes that she was duped into believing that she was saved, based upon what ultimately did occur. While on vacation a year ago in an airplane, this churchgoin woman was headed for Los Vegas to gamble no less. While 35,000 feet in the air, the Holy Ghost "breathed" on her. That's right. She got saved on the airplane. In a split second, she got convicted of sin and new life entered into her. No longer a gambler since that eventful day, she knows without a doubt that she is now SAVED. She herself had nothing to do with it. Nor did her church. It was ALL the Holy Ghost. He could have saved her in church, but He didn't. Not for 20 years. Hear the serious warning of the founder and leader of Deliverance Counseling Center:

> *If I were not a "front line warrior," driven out of the comfort zone of the organized church, I too would be as ignorant of Satan's devices as anyone else. Simply put, my impressions are based on one solid fact that I experience through my daily contacts on the web and through telephone counseling. The bottom line is that people are just not getting saved in church---no matter the size, the denomination, the non- denomination, even the country, people are not getting saved in church. And I am counseling and praying with people who have sat under the ministries of well known, tv mega preachers. Believe me, the size of the altar call response DOES NOT MATTER. No one is being saved by motivational, inspirational preaching, or by the prosperity gospel. As Jesus warned, what does it profit a man to gain the whole world, yet lose his own soul? Heed the words of the Lord Jesus Christ, "Come Out of Her My People lest you receive of her plagues.!"*

FALSE FIRE

Unfortunately, very few churchgoers who declare that they are "word" people rarely ever study history. A part of rightly dividing the word is to interpret its meaning in accordance with the most relevant historical perspective. Simply put, we need to stop randomly selecting scriptures out of context and ascertain the whats, whens and the wherefores regarding what was going on at the time that the word was written and what has transpired since. For example, many believers misunderstand that just because being born again involves "old things being passed away," how will we be able to assess our spiritual growth today, if we don't consider "how we used to be?" Along these same lines, the real truth about the influence of the Jezebel spirit in our times can be traced to its historic roots that go back a century or so ago.

Consequently, to discern the signs of the times, we need to understand "what went on yesterday, particularly about 100 years ago. Since a good tree doesn't bring forth bad fruit and a bad tree doesn't bring forth good fruit---we should be able to know ourselves today by the fruit of yesterday. Calling down fire from heaven is an endtimes sign that is to be manifested by the beast in the book of Revelation. Is this actual or is this metaphorical? Here are the reasons why we believe this sign to be symbolic. In the old testament, the only human being who could call down fire from heaven was Elijah and he did so on more than one occasion.

In one case, Elijah called down actual fire from heaven as a military stand against his enemies, the prophets of Baal. On yet another occasion, Elijah demonstrated the superiority of God in comparison to the gods of the prophets of Baal. The god called Baal was merely a religious demon in the service of Satan. In a contest between Elijah and Satan's prophets, the enemy repeatedly tried to "call down fire from heaven" without any success. However, Elijah prayed and God answered his prayer by sending down actual fire from heaven to consume the offering on the altar. So our point of view is that Satan's workers could not literally accomplish this feat or they would have done so in the contest with Elijah. Logically speaking, the fire called down from heaven by "the beast of endtimes" MUST BE "a false fire."

We are warned by the Lord Jesus Christ that in the end times there will be a huge outpouring of false miracles, signs and wonders that will deceive much of the Christian world. Mark 13:22 "For false Christs and false prophets shall rise, and shall shew signs and wonders, to seduce, if it were possible, even the elect." Jesus implied with His statement "if it were possible," that it is practically impossible to deceive "forever" the elect once they have been saved, yet it CAN be done!

In the first instance, each and every one of the elect was deceived "prior" to the Holy Ghost calling us to truth and therefore the Lord's strategy has been to "un-deceive" us enough so that He can save us. He used just two nuggets of truth to win us all: that we must repent and that Jesus Christ was raised from the dead. Then there is a second group---those who have been deceived AFTER they became born again. Consider just two counterfeits: "slain in the spirit" and speaking in "a prayer language." Yet if the deceived among the elect would simply cry out to Lord in prayer and ask " Father, show me the truth.," the Lord will uncover the deception speedily.

Moreover, we believe that even the delusions that cloud the minds and hearts of the elect in this hour are yet another sign that we are approaching the end of the endtimes. In short, too many of the elect of God are deceived today. "The Fake Jesus" has targeted the elect by deceiving them with false signs and wonders. Our goal is to draw your attention to the fact that many of the events predicted for the end times are now occurring. Yet you may be surprised to learn that in the 19th century, many believed that "the endtimes" would occur in their generation. Ironically, for this reason, certain leaders of that day expected that God was going to restore miracles, divine healing and other signs and wonders to the church, in order to usher in the return of the Lord.

Yet, in the history of this planet, no generation has ever before seen such a continuously increasing amount of natural disasters like earthquakes and forest fires, as well as an explosion in technological capabilities such as the world wide web. Nor has the survival of world's population been more ominously threatened to t as in our own times. We are not trying to convince anyone of a time line for end time events because we do not have one. We will not make the same mistake as did 19th century Christians and others do today. We believe that the tribulation began with the first world war and could yet continue for another 50 years or more before "the end."

Nevertheless, even to the non-Christian and the least informed spiritually, significant signs are pointing toward the soon coming of the Lord, and as such we need to hearken to the severe and clear warning that the disciple Mark gave to us. As such, we need to be aware that false signs and miracles are even today occurring. Not only should we earnestly search the scriptures so as to be able to discern the true from the counterfeit, but we must also look to church history for some answers.

Within this context, how do we define the new term heard frequently in recent months---the Christian euphemism called "FALSE FIRE!?" Simply put and in a nutshell, false fire is the counterfeit of the ministry of the Holy Ghost. It also signifies the need within man to experience the presence of God in a sensual, emotional way and thereby exercise both his senses and his emotions to "manufacture" sensationalism, in the form of signs and wonders, including but not limited to healings, miracles and prophecies.

We anticipate your question. "How do we know if we have accepted a counterfeit or a mixed doctrine?" The answer is rather simple. Jesus very clearly yet profoundly tells us how "to know." He basically tells us to "examine the root." A good tree will not produce evil fruit. And an evil tree will not produce good fruit. And---we know them by their fruit. This is the sheer magnitude of the importance of studying church history. For within the reports of our ancestors, lies the evidence as to whether the "tree" of the generations that preceded us planted either good or evil seed. It is apparent that all of us who live TODAY are a part of the church at Laodicea. If our supposition is correct--- that we are ALL Laodicean Christians--- then it is not a stretch of logical reasoning to expect that there are some manifestations of "false fire" among us.

In our studies, we have noted that the age of the church at Philadelphia gave way to the beginning of the Laodicean church age in the year 1830. Besides the first generation church symbolized by the church at Ephesus, we have seen strong indications that the church at Philadelphia began with the Protestant Reformation that was founded by Martin Luther and others in 1517. Around 1830, the church dispensation of Philadelphia began to phase out and the church at Laodicea slowly but consistently emerged. Error began to creep into the foundational truths, permeating like yeast both Christian doctrine, traditions and practices. Consequently, the Laodicean Age didn't just begin with the prosperity gospel and the mega preachers of the 20th and 21 centuries. This is why a study of church history is so important to our understanding of where we now stand.

DIVINE HEALING

Simply put, a review of church history reveals that the seeds of what is going on now in "charismania" were planted in the early 19th century. Actually, the concentration on divine healing has a longer history than does the speaking in other tongues. As in our own times, false fire of the 19th century also led to spectacular crowds as well as confusion and turmoil within the churches in those days. While tongues came to the forefront in 1901 in the ministries of Charles Parham in Topeka Kansas amd William Seymore's Azusa Street Revival in Los Angeles in 1906, the emphasis on divine healing goes back to the mid 1800's as a result of efforts being made to restore signs and wonders to the church. In 1901, Parham is also the one who formulated the doctrine of speaking in tongues as the "initial evidence" of the baptism of the Holy Ghost.

Nevertheless, the roots of all modern healing movements originated in Europe: Edward Irving in London(1830), Johann Blumhart in Germany (1843), Dorothea Trudel in Switzerland (1851) and Otto Stockmayer in Switzerland. (1867) To learn more about their lives and ministries, we suggest that you do as we did. Search the web with their names. In the USA, even though healing was practiced by Joseph Smith of the Mormons and Elizabeth Mix, an African American Holiness evangelist, the first person to bring healing to America on a more widespread basis was himself a physician, Charles Cullis of Boston. Cullis began by adding prayer to his practice of traditional medicine. By 1870, a patient named Lucy Drake was instantly healed of a brain tumor after hands were layed on her---a situation that caused Cullis to set aside medicine in favor of divine healing.

By 1901, Parham also opened a "healing home" where prayer and bible reading took the place of doctors and medicine. As for Seymore of Azusa Street in LA, he opened the door to some extreme beliefs within the divine healing movement. When questioned as to whether or not taking medicine was wrong for a Christian, Seymore answered in the affirmative, claiming that medicine is for the unbeliever, but the remedy for the saints was faith in the atonement because the Lord has given ALL Christians power over sickness and disease. From Seymore's Azusa Street Revival to World War II, Pentecostals made headlines in many communities over extreme views and practices regarding divine healing, most noteworthy among them was Alexander Dowie. Dowie and several others were tried and convicted of manslaughter for letting family members die for lack of medical attention.

In 1948, Oral Roberts continued the divine healing tradition, claiming to be commissioned by God to bring God's healing power to his generation. In fact, Roberts is the first TV evangelist, as he had his healing lines nationally televised in 1953. Kathryn Kuhlman (1907-1976) was also a well known TV evangelist. As a part of our research, we reviewed some of Kuhlman's bio and we came away with an impression that she was sincere, but that she preached some significant error concerning the Holy Ghost and the rapture.

Therefore, it is quite possible that without knowledge of hypnotism and other forms of occultism, Kuhlman was a primary target for demonic deception. In 1973, Benny Hinn attended one of Kuhlman's healing crusades. Contact with Kuhlman was a significant catalyst for Hinn's ministry---and he too, continues to spread all of Kuhlman's error throughout the global television network and worldwide crusades. He even claims to have "received the power" as he cried out for it at Kuhlman's gravesite--clear and convincing evidence of necromancy at work.

"THE 'MAKE A DECISION" GOSPEL"

Hand and hand with spreading the error of the 19th century, though not known for divine healing was Charles Finney.(1792-1875) *A fiery New York preacher, Finney's impact on church traditions and practices in the United States was so profound, that his influence is still spreading globally, more than 100 years after his death. Finney's notoriety is that he is the one who brought into the entire church the practice of "make a decision for Christ" through repeating the sinners prayer, the altar call, and counting converts.*

A practicing freemason for 8 years, although Finney eventually DID disavowed it, we have learned in our work that those who were ever deeply involved in this brand of witchcraft very often require a "hands on" deliverance to be completely set free which we suspect that Finney did not receive. Finney enflamed yet another false fire through the global church practice that employs the invitation system and the altar call to evoke an emotional response, where people are not worshiping in spirit and in truth, but in the flesh and in error... The invitation system seeks to condition and even manipulate people for emotional reactions that ignite a false fire.

The tools of the seduction include uplifting, often energetic, even tribal, rhythmic type music with lots of percussion instruments, dynamic personalities who prance, shout and strut themselves across the platform---in other words, a charged up atmosphere "by any means necessary". The problem with this sort of worship is that it tends to provoke an emotional, demonstrative response---an outburst so to speak---- that is based on factors other than the truth of the gospel of Jesus crucified, dead, buried, raised, ascended and coming back. Dynamic preachers of all denominations and persuasions can be extremely skilled at manipulating a crowd by stirring up the emotions of people. When the emotions of a congregation are stirred, the shouts, screams and similar outcries can light a false fire throughout the congregation, the results of which are erroneously attributed to an outpouring of the Holy Ghost.

"Holy" laughter, "holy"dancing, shouting, falling out slain, rolling on the floor, running up and down the aisles, throwing money at the feet of prominent evangelists and other forms of emotional frenzy keep the false flame alive. At these euphoric times, not only are the pockets and wallets fleeced, but people "get high" and think to themselves "now is the time I can give myself to Jesus" and they start marching down aisles in small churches and in big tents, convention halls and stadiums. Not to be misunderstood regarding worship, we certainly do not suggest that reverent music and praise has no place , but rather, no emotional tactic needs to be employed to psychologically condition sinners to come forward to the altar and "confess Christ". If the elect are assembled within the assembly, the Holy Ghost knows how to reach them once they have heard the simplicity of the gospel. The problem is that the messages or sermons that accompany theatrical antics of preachers are often not grounded in the gospel of Jesus Christ.

Here is how Satan operates with the false fire of healing. Once you think of it, it is really not that clever but the reason why this particular tactic "works" is because we are so gullible in our fleshly desire to look for signs to prove to us that God is real when what we are called to do is live by faith, without needing a sign to believe in Him. As Jesus said, "a perverse generation seeks after a sign." In conjunction with the ultimate ramifications of sin and death upon our un-glorified, natural bodies, Satan DOES use sickness and disease to promote his own agenda. God uses it as well for His own reasons. An important last days component of Satan's agenda is to fool the elect. So what better way to fool us then with a divine healing hoax? All it takes is for the demon to withdraw the symptoms of the sickness from those whom he made sick in the first place!!! Unfortunately, the sickness itself is not gone. Only the symptoms are gone or in medical terms "put into remission" in order to fulfill an even higher agenda which is allowing a demon spirit to imitate God.

Once we took a closer look at the 19th century, we have a different perspective on the mega preachers of today. It could be that like Kathryn Kuhlman, some of them are NOT false prophets. The pattern that we noticed in each and every case is that ONE event served as the catalyst for a total shift in direction and purpose. For Kathryn Kuhlman, born to Baptist and Methodist parents---her significant day occurred while preaching a traditional sermon when suddenly her message was interrupted by "spontaneous healings" throughout the congregation.

Perhaps one of the most perverse sermons that we have ever heard preached was called "Divine Release." The sermon was presented by Juanita Bynum-Weeks a few years ago. It was absolutely horrendous. Yet, Juanita first came to public attention by the preaching of ONE noteworthy message called "No More Sheets." Bynum's message was more of an emotional, personal testimony about her struggles with fornication as a single Christian woman then it was a traditional sermon. Yet this one televised opportunity provided by TD Jakes changed the complete direction of Juanita's life just as Jakes' life was forever changed once TBN's founder, Paul Crouch watched a homemade video featuring n TD Jakes .

Is Juanita Bynum a false prophet? To be honest, there is only one thing that we are sure of. Bynum is the fruit that fell from the tree of Pentecostalism whose roots are embedded not only in her home church but also entrenched within the church influences of the 19th century. We believe that Pentecostalism is an evil tree that was planted by sincere, yet sincerely wrong people and we ALL have been affected by it. Whether by vision, prophecy, a manifestation of a sign or a wonder, our findings are that sincere and gifted Christian leaders simply "took a wrong turn" a century ago that spread like a wild fire, defiling all others who followed them.

Sincerity aside, some mega preachers took the wrong turn primarily because their narcissistic personalities were never broken by the cross. So it was natural for them to allow prominence, prosperity and power to develop huge ministerial systems that are built around their own self love and "mega" pride. Some less than sincere prophets gather to fill their own pockets and serve their own perversion for domination, manipulation and control. The bottom line is that it is the Lord's intent to undeceive the sincere believers within the Laodicean church age. Consequently, we all have a great price to pay when we face the light of truth and discover that much of our work and effort has merely opened a door of opportunity to the fake Jesus.

As we have searched for answers and solutions, we are truly dumbfounded by the mercy, grace and longsuffering of our God. It literally amazes us to attempt to comprehend that for centuries, even going back to the rebellious children of Israel in the old testament, the Lord has tolerated mixed and false doctrines of all kinds for centuries on end. Yet, throughout the history of God's people, He has STILL used those who spread mixed and false doctrines to evangelize and teach the gospel of Jesus Christ. Think of it!!!! Just based upon the fact that the Lord has tolerated false fire for so long should suggest to us that "we are near the end."

So was David right? Does God's mercy endure forever? To that scripture, we may shock you by answering both "yes" and "no." On a broad scale, one of God's eternal character traits is to be merciful and longsuffering. However, the Book of Revelation is a clear warning to us all that an end to God's patience is definitely coming. We anticipate that the organized church shall soon be awakened to this sobering fact. So we warn you the reader -----that as the Holy Ghost begins to move to wake up and un-deceive the elect, make sure that you are NOT trusting in tv ministries, church attendance and manifestations of FALSE FIRE.

Remembering the fervor of the early 80's, the word of faith movement clearly "took off" primarily because of tongues. Everyone was seeking the initial sign of the baptism in the Holy Ghost, as word of faith preachers, pastors and teachers all concurred that tongues was the initial evidence. At times, seeking after uttering a tongue seemed higher in priority than even the salvation of souls, as the leaders taught that being saved was only a beginning step to being "filled." Consequently, those who proclaimed to be "born again" did not settle for conversion alone because being filled with the Holy Spirit meant that "you spoke in tongues."

Those who are in opposition to the gifts of the Spirit often declare that tongues and the rest of the gifts of the Holy Ghost have ceased. Prior to the early 20th century, history would suggest that the speaking in tongues actually DID cease for several centuries. While the Middle Ages constituted long years of spiritual darkness, the Protestant Reformation exemplified a revelatory outburst of light regarding the doctrines of sin, salvation, justification by faith and holiness. This period marked the interpretation of scripture by some of the finest minds in church history. Even though there were some instances of "the ecstatic" among a group called the Anabaptists, for the most part, the Reformation was silent about the speaking in tongues.

Moreover, within the founding days of America, neither the Pilgrims, the Puritan leaders, nor any other Christian group indulged in speaking in tongues. Times of great emotional conviction were recorded and believers were moved to show their convictions through their fervency of feelings and emotions. Yet, even though thousands were convicted of their sins in frontier revivals, the speaking in tongues found no expression. Earnest Christians and ministers in this period of history set themselves to re-discover truth. Literary Christian scholars produced excellent essays and formulated studious, insightful exegetical scriptural interpretations, yet not one spiritual leader of the Reformation period in the USA even intimated that the doctrine of speaking in tongues had any role at all in the spiritual life of that day.

Our study of church history reveals that the Jezebel spirit is a religious demon that began to empower some key human players, both male and female. These professing Christians unknowingly began to insidiously defile the church with errors that have spread to such an extent that truth became mixed with lies and formed a spiritual perversion. Here is how it all got started. In the third decade of the 19th century, a pastor in London by the name of Edward Irving made a public declaration of healing, prophecies and tongues, including them in his worship services. Upon visiting Irving's church, contemporary essayists wrote in the London Times, "God was working miracles by hysterics." Though Irving was ousted from the Presbyterian Church, he started another, namely, the Catholic Apostolic Church.

A spiritual truth that bare repeating once again, Jesus gave us a simple tool of discernment. He tells us that good trees produce good fruit, bad trees produce bad fruit, and that we "know them by their fruit." The Lord made it clear that a bad tree cannot produce good fruit. As we continued to study, we found that the precursors of the pentecostal movement which centered itself in the speaking in tongues was filled with "bad fruit." Let's look at the lives and work of each outstanding leader, one at a time. Although the spirit of Jezebel used men like Irving, it is particularly attracted to women. It is interesting to note the significant influence of women in the tongues movement and the establishment of the denomination of Pentecostalism.

Here is a summary of a few men and women who were deceived by Jezebel more than 100 years ago:

Mother Ann Lee" founder of the Shakers, 1736-1784: Mother Lee was the charismatic founder of the United Society of Believers in Christ's Second Appearing, commonly known as the Shakers. After a difficult early life, she joined a group of Christians in Manchester, England, who had split from the Quaker movement. Their unorthodox views and impassioned convulsions in worship drew ridicule and persecution, along with the nickname "the Shakers." While imprisoned,

Mother Ann received a revelation that she was the embodiment of the second coming of Christ, in feminine form. Lee claimed that she could also discourse in 72 tongues. Lee settled in Watervliet New York.

Joseph Smith, the founder of the Mormons, 1805-1844: Smith was among the first to advocate for the speaking in tongues. He believed that tongues opens the door to visions and revelations. After all, this is the way that the book of Mormon had come to him. Taken from a chronological history of the Mormon church, is the following excerpt:

> History of the Church 2:428, 27 March 1836: [at the end of the temple dedication] "President Brigham Young gave a short address in tongues, and David W. Patten interpreted, and gave a short exhortation in tongues himself, after which I [Joseph Smith] blessed the congregation in the name of the Lord, and the assembly dispersed a little past four o'clock, having manifested the most quiet demeanor during the whole exercise....
> During the evening of the same day, Brother George A. Smith arose and began to prophesy, when a noise was heard like the sound of a rushing mighty wind, which filled the Temple, and all the congregation simultaneously arose, being moved upon by an invisible power; many began to speak in tongues and prophesy; others saw glorious visions;
> I beheld the Temple was filled with angels which fact I declared to the congregation. The people of the neighborhood came running together (hearing an unusual sound within, and seeing a bright light like a pillar of fire resting upon the Temple), and were astonished at what was taking place. This continued until the

meeting closed at eleven p. m."

To discern what we have just read, let us bare in mind what John Smith and the Mormons believe about Jesus Christ of Nazareth: They preach that Jesus is the brother of Satan, an elder brother of all people on this planet. Mormons teach that Jesus was born on an unnamed planet near the star kolob through God the Father having sex with one of his many wives. In short, that the Lord was born on Earth through God manifesting a body and having sex with Mary. They claim that Jesus was married to three women at the same time, and had children. Consider yet another outrage Mormon teaching, namely, that Jesus saved himself by obeying the principals of Mormonism and that the Lord is an example for all good Mormons to follow. John Smith also claimed that Jesus received godhood after he rose from the dead and that He is now one of many gods over his own planet with his many wives making spirit babies and populating that planet.

Since the fruit does not fall far from the tree, when we consider that the founder of this outrageous idolatry is one of the first Americans to proclaim that he "spoke in tongues," are spiritual eyebrows should be raised. Assuming that what John Smith wrote in the Mormon history book about the supernatural manifestation that occurred in his gatherings, ask yourself this. Based upon John Smith's blasphemous doctrine, "was the Holy Spirit the author of that experience on March 27, 1836???????? The obvious answer to the question is a resounding "NO!"

Marie Woodworth Etter, faith healing and evangelist: (1844-1924) is one of the best known Holiness preachers of the pre-Pentecostal era. From around 1885 onwards she began to use the charismatic gifts in her meetings, and was known for healings, trances and visions. Licensed to preach in 1884, Etter was the mega preacher of her day in tent revivals. Her critics called her "the Voodoo Priestess." She was known for speaking in tongues, along with strange and sundry manifestations that were attributed to the movement of the Holy Ghost. Etter was was also known for preaching texts out of context, preached regularly for the Mormons, and seemed to be the person who started the phenomena known today as "slain in the spirit." Most of the manifestations common in present day meetings like the Toronto Blessing were experienced in the Woodworth-Etter meetings, so much so that some critics of the current movement trace The Toronto blessing back to Etter. Etter was certainly faithful to her calling and it appears that she was honest and sincere. But as Pam points out in "Faces of the Religious Demon", "we are now living in an era when the Lord will turn over those with a religious demon to a reprobate mind. At that moment, the captive's thoughts will be permanently darkened to the degree that he becomes incapable of receiving the truth." (pg 47)

Charles Parham, founder of pentecostalism, 1873-1929 is an extremely controversial figure. We recommend to those who are interested to search the web with his name and read about him for yourself. There are rumors of homosexuality, racism, (membership in the Klu Klux Klan) and freemasonry. He was actually arrested for lewdness in a public place, attempting to solicit sex from men. Moreover, there are also several allegations and reports concerning his strange doctrinal interpretations. In regards to tongues, in the fall of 1900, after leading his students through a series of Bible studies on repentance, justification by faith, sanctification, and healing, Parham instructed them on Spirit baptism. By the end of December, they were prepared to encounter the day of Pentecost in a new way.

After the revival commenced on New Year's Day, Parham announced that the students had spoken many languages. He himself claimed he had received the capability of preaching in German and Swedish. On January 1, 1901, Agnes Ozman spoke in a tongue that sounded like "Chinese," though never actually verified. She is renowned as being the first pentecostal person to ever speak in tongues. The problem with her tongue speaking is that it is claimed that she spoke non stop for 3 days in Chinese, actually unable to speak in English until she was "released" to do so.

Others among Parham's students were alleged to have spoken in a variety of languages including Japanese, Hungarian, Syrian, Hindi, and Spanish. Parham noted that "cloven tongues of fire" appeared over the heads of the speakers. Sometimes interpretations followed such as "God is love," "Jesus is mighty to save," and "Jesus is ready to hear." Parham anticipated that he could send out missionaries all over the world who would supernaturally speak in the native tongue of the land, without having studied it. It never happened and Parham was extremely disappointed that his missionary plans were thwarted. Although Parham was accused of being a racist, he preferred to consider himself a separationist, as exemplified by the fact that he allowed a black man to participate in his bible study classes, sitting in a restricted and separated part of the study hall.

That man was William Seymour, a waiter and the Azusa Street leader (1870-1922) Seymour went to Los Angeles and taught the Holy Spirit baptism in a warehouse on Azusa Street. On 4/ 4, 1906 a revival began and thousand's of people came to 312 Azusa to receive the baptism in the Holy Spirit. This revival lasted from 1906-1913, and during this time, thousands of Pentecostal missionaries went forth establishing missions throughout the world. Seymour's work at Azusa is regarded among most Pentecostal historians as a genuine move of God in restoring the church to true power and authority. However, it has also been reported that the Azusa Street meetings were filled with spiritualist mediums, hypnotists, and others who had a deep interest in the occult. There are reports of fits, babblings, jerks, twitchings, shakings, as well mass hysteria. In fact, the spiritual pandemonium of the meetings led to moral compromise with people falling on top of each other. Ultimately more than Seymour could handle alone, he sent for his teacher, Parham to come and help out.

When Parham arrived, he was outraged and appalled. As a result, Parham and Seymour had a rift that was never reconciled. Parham publicly denounced both the revival and Seymour in October 1906 for the emotionalism displayed in the worship at the Azusa Street revival, and for the intermingling of blacks and whites in the services. Seymour had sought Parham to help him control these ecstatic excesses. But visiting the mission for the first time and observing what Parham believed to be "manifestations of the flesh," Parham stood up and declared: "God is sick at His stomach!"

Even so, it is reported that emotionalism played a strong part in Parham's own worship services. This unfortunate incident and his judgmental nature alienated Parham not only from Seymour, but others as well. It is alleged without substantiation that Seymour "stole Parham's pentecostal movement" by blackmail as Seymour was privy to Parham's secret sex life. Shortly, the pentecostal movement had now begun to move well beyond both men. In fact, Pentecostalism emerged in India in 1906 among holiness believers without ties to Azusa Street.

Another prominent evangelist of the period was **Evan Roberts and The Wales Revival of 1904-1905.** A significant part of the appeal of this widescale revival lay in Evan Roberts himself, a charismatic and sincere preacher. Although he came from the Welsh Methodist tradition, he wasn't a theologian, and he never finished his training to be a minister. His message was for all the people of Wales, regardless of denomination, and it was immensely appealing. Meetings would be a mixture of prayer, self examination and singing, and they could last for hours. The most outstanding aspect of the revival was its impact upon everyday societal life. Crime dropped, saloons closed, in short, the entire community was affected. It is believed that at least 100,000 people became Christians during the 1904-1905 revival, but despite this, the revival did not put a stop to the gradual decline of Christianity in Wales, only holding it back slightly.

It has been argued by some Christian historians that the 1904-1905 revival lacked depth in terms of nurturing the newly converted Christians in biblical teaching. Evan Roberts admitted that wildfire erupted "from the very outset." He reported that the physical, mental, and spiritual wreckage resulting from the baptism in the Holy Ghost was appalling in its effect upon the revival's leaders and workers, to say nothing of the new converts.

It is also reported that "thousands," and, "nearly all," were "wrecked." Such a destructive outcome should lead us to obviously question whether or not this revival was from God. If it was, why did Evan Roberts himself suffer a severe mental breakdown at the end of the revival, from which he never recovered? As a result, the public ministry of Evan Roberts was finished. He recuperated at the home of perhaps the most outstanding minister of the last century, Jessie Penn Lewis, a renowned woman of God. In fact, Evans assisted Lewis in writing "War on the Saints." Nevertheless, when the book was denounced by critics in that day, it is reported that Roberts denied co-authoring it.

Jessie Penn Lewis, author of "War on the Saints." ((1861-1927) was an English evangelical speaker and author of a number of Christian evangelical works. Her father was a Calvinist Methodist minister. Along with Evan Roberts, Penn Lewis was significantly involved in the 1904-1905 Welsh Revival. As previously noted, the revival was abruptly shortened with the mental and physical collapse of Evan Roberts. Penn-Lewis traveled internationally to take her spiritual warfare message to audiences in Russia, Scandinavia, Canada, the U.S., and India. She has remained a controversial figure among Christians for almost 100 years, primarily because she declared the failure of the

Welsh Revival to be the work of Satan. Emphasis is centered in "War on the Saints" of the danger that comes to believers at the point of baptism in the Holy Ghost, yet little reference is made to tongues. In a subtitled called "The Counterfeit Presence is Sensual," Penn-Lewis writes: (War on the Saints, pg. 130-131)

> "The counterfeit presence of God is given by deceiving spirits, working upon the physical frame, or within the bodily frame, upon the senses. We have seen the beginning of this, and how the first ground is gained. It is deepened by these sense-manifestations being repeated, so gently, that the man goes on yielding to them, thinking this is truly 'communion with God'---- for believers too often look upon 'communion with God' as a thing of sense and not of spirit--- and here he commences praying to evil spirits under the belief that he is praying to God.
>
> The self control is not yet lost, but as the believer responds to, or gives himself up to these 'conscious' manifestations, he does not know that his **WILLPOWER IS BEING SLOWLY UNDERMINED.**
> At last through these subtle, delicious experiences, the faith is established that God Himself is CONSCIOUSLY IN POSSESSION OF THE BODY, quickening it with felt thrills of life, or filling it with warmth and heat, or even 'agonies' which seem like fellowship with the sufferings of Christ, and travail for souls, or the experience of death with Christ in the consciousness of nails being driven into the bodily frame, etc. From this point, the lying spirits (demons) can work as they will, and there is no limit as to what they may do to a

believer deceived to this extent. (Jessie Penn-Lewis)

Almost a century ago, this remarkable woman of God wrote words that describe us today! From the agonies and travail for souls, the feelings of warmth and heat, the consciousness of nails being driven into the bodily frame, most charismatics have experienced all of this---proving that there is nothing new under the sun where the religious demon is concerned. He just reworks the same ole stuff. In "War on the Saints" a short paragraph can be found accompanied by a specific footnote toward the end of the book regarding tongues in small print which is quoted below:

> "A question arises here as to whether believers may now speak in unknown tongues, as the disciples did at the time of the Holy Spirit's infilling at Pentecost. There are those that say 'Yes" but the truths set forth in preceding chapters, show that until the spiritual section of the Church of Christ are more acquainted with the counterfeiting methods of the spirits of evil, and the laws which give them power of working, any testimony to such experience AS TRUE, cannot be safely relied upon. (pg. 298)

And here is the footnote that is written below in fine print in War on the Saints:

> **The subject of speaking in tongues is not further dealt with, as the counterfeits in connection with it are only a fraction of the countless counterfeits being forced upon the children of God AT THE PRESENT TIME, numbers of which are not referred to in these pages. A believer not deceived by counterfeit**

> speaking in tongues can be deceived and possessed by accepting other counterfeits. An understanding of the BROAD PRINCIPLES showing the basic differences between the way of God's working, and the deceptive imitations by Satan, will enable spiritual believers to discern for themselves all the counterfeits they meet with today.

Clearly, Jessie Penn-Lewis was more concerned about "her day and time" then she was about ours. Having ministered in the most well known revival that has occurred in recorded church history since the days of the early church, much of her wisdom comes from experience. Likewise, our own reservations about tongues are primarily connected to our findings relative to counseling professing Christians for deliverance. We have discovered that the vast majority of these captives also speak in tongues, yet their torment is an indication that some have also been seriously demonized.

Evidently, Penn-Lewis was not a prophet and therefore, the Lord did not show her "our times" or perhaps she would have spent more time on the speaking in tongues--a practice that has evolved in this hour into a major controversy. In spite of the historical perspective, we have not yet come to the conclusion that tongues has permanently ceased. The Lord may have another use for it that we are yet unaware of. Our concern does not rule out a bonafide manifestation but our focus is on the counterfeit. As such, we agree with our contemporary, Dr. Rebecca Brown's warning concerning counterfeits manifested through the speaking in other tongues. Her comments were made relative to charismatic Catholics but Dr. Brown's words apply to word of faith followers and those within pentecostal denominations as well:

> "Christians have made the terrible mistake of assuming that ALL tongues are from God. How

> wrong they are!...It is well known that many occultic rituals are done in tongues ...The fact that Catholics speak in tongues is not proof that they are filled with the Holy Spirit. Too many of these precious Catholic souls assume that because they are speaking in tongues, they are saved. How can the Holy Spirit be operative and manifesting in a system of idolatry?"(Preparefor War, pgs 182-3)

In a nutshell, Dr. Brown's rhetorical question is the bottom line, because she has addressed the overriding issue. Therefore, we must concur that we do not believe that tongues and its interpretation can be a gift from God within an idolatrous system. The degeneration of the organized church system in the last two decades or more has now gone wild with the prosperity gospel. The amount of money pilfered from unsuspecting, faithful people in tithes and offerings is beyond our imagination to even attempt to calculate. Furthermore, the current segment of the charismatic/pentecostal system's preaching of faith and divine healing has seriously injured and caused premature death to countless of people who have refused needed medical attention that could have spared their lives.

Yet the tragedies of today are actually influenced by the ministries of Parham and another 19th century minister--- John Alexander Dowey. Called the Father of Healing Revivalism, Dowey was arrested and charged with manslaughter in the death of his own daughter, who died from a severe burn due to Dowey's refusal to seek medical attention on her behalf. The beat goes on as we have recently watched video and television documentaries of people whose deceased relatives believed in error that they were healed at a Benny Hinn crusade and very recently, Todd Bentley meetings. Only God Himself knows how many of his children on their death beds suffered needlessly,----depressed because some word of faith preacher taught them that anyone who becomes sick has either failed God or that their faith in God was too weak to be healed by Him.

So how can anyone with a sound mind trust a system that has been replete with error for 100 years? We have searched the scriptures and we have reviewed the history of tongues. Our studies have confirmed that most of what we see operative today in tongues is counterfeit. Yet, we continue to seek the Holy Ghost to reveal to us whether or not there remains a legitimate manifestation of the gift of speaking in tongues in our time. Our founder has experienced a use of tongues that is not recorded in the bible nor in church history. Therefore, she remains very cautious because she does not want to become another Parham--starting a new practice that opens the door to even more demons. We reiterate that that just because much of the organized church is uttering a counterfeit tongue does NOT negate that there may very well be a legitimate, true use of tongues today. If there is a true gift of tongues in operation, we should be privy to know how to discern the true gift from the fake one. Likewise, if tongues has actually ceased by the hand of God, we should not attempt to restore it.

CHAPTER EIGHT

So What Happens Now?

Simply stated, it's any discerning believer's guess! We suspect that it is quite possible that the organized church has already been judged relatively recently, perhaps decades, maybe even a century ago. If not, then judgment is very close at hand. It seems that Satan began to progressively establish a seat within church divisions, sects, and organizations since around the third century. Therefore, it stands to reason that the book of Revelation was written to and for every church age.

However, death has been a real blessing for the saints who have already left this earth prior to "the end." Truly, those who are alive when the Lord Jesus Christ returns for the dead and the living will face a challenge that no other church age has been required to face. We believe that we are very close to that hour NOW---as we live in the best of times and the worst of times. Those who are over 70 may see the grave, maybe NOT----but their children and certainly their grandchildren may yet be alive when both the Fake Jesus and the True Jesus comes. According to second Thessalonians, we know that the Fake Jesus will come FIRST.

So where do we stand now?

Today we are in the midst of a transition. Pam reflects upon an interesting personal experience in the summer of 1981, and recent inspired revelation called "the parable of the condemned building:

> I sat in a chair dozing,--(not asleep yet not fully awake either,) I heard the audible voice of the Lord. I didn't have to try the spirits on this one. Didn't have a chance to. He said "Pam," and my spirit caused my mouth to answer immediately--- "Yes, Lord." Then He said "I am

about to do a new thing with My Church." I stirred, stretched a bit and answered, " Uh, huh." Then, in the sweetest voice I have ever heard in my life, He asked very politely, without a hint of command or demand----
"Can I use you??"

I was spiritually ignorant back then and so I answered without even thinking, "Sure Lord. Let's start with the Roses of Hope." It took years for me to realize that "His church" was not just the local church that I was a member of. In my local church, The Roses of Hope was a money raising group who organized house parties where they had card games and sold liquor to raise money for the church. I had only been a churchgoer for two years in 1981 when I received a call to ministry.. Likewise, I was still as carnal as the rest of the members, but commonsense told me that there was something not quite right about THIS kind of money raising. Once I mentioned the Roses of Hope, my conversation with the Lord stopped immediately and there was a deep silence. Disappointed, I thought to myself "what did I say that turned Him off?" I was such a babe.

I have heard His voice a few times since **but never again quite LIKE THAT!!!** Looking back, I realize that this encounter with the Lord was one of the several ways that I received my calling 26 years ago prior to entering the ministry on Oct. 25, 1981. At that time, I did not know what a sermon was much less a calling to ministry, so it took at least 10 signs for me to finally comprehend that I was being called. Even so, I have never forgotten the Lord's mentioning of "the new thing." So what is the new thing that the Lord is going to do with "His Church?" In 26 years, I can honestly tell you that I do not yet know for sure, but there have been some signs and indications. I received one noteworthy sign in August 2007. I had yet another "conversation." There was no audible voice this time, as the communication was from " the sender of the message to my spirit and then to my mind." At the time, I was attempting to set up a conference schedule to conduct deliverance training seminars for a local church leader and I ran into a "closed door." Almost immediately, the Lord revealed to me that He was the one who closed the door.

Wondering why, I sought the Father in prayer. It didn't take long for me to be answered. In less than a week, a kind of telepathic communication took place to let me know that I was "on the wrong track". I didn't even have a chance to emotionally respond to the unexpected rejection I had recently experienced. Once I understood that it was God Himself who had "hardened hearts", I completely changed my direction and I forgot about the particular "friend" in ministry that stood in my way. I realized that God used her to "close the door.". It has been revealed to my spirit that my ministry is not to equip or edify the traditional church, certainly NOT on church property.

My answer came through a kind of parable. I was asked, "would you put up curtains at the windows of a condemned building?" I answered with my mind. "No." Then a kind of a speech was made that went something like this. "A homeless person will make a home in a condemned building. To escape the elements of the weather on the outside, he will satisfy himself and "make do" with no heat, no running water, no lights, and he will share his dwelling with the occupants: the rats and the roaches." Then I was hit in the face with this statement. "If you try to edify the organized church with seminars and conferences, you will be putting up curtains at the windows of a condemned building."

Wow! I was stunned. Metaphorically speaking, it was clear to me that the condemned building was a symbol of the organized church. If this "mental conversation" was from the Holy Ghost)===== then the metaphor is suggesting that the organized church is a condemned building. Please note that I am still trying the spirits, so I am not saying "thus says the Lord" in this instance. Condemnation suggests "judgment." The word says that "judgment will begin at the household of faith." Therefore, natural logic by simple commonsense suggests to me that "the organized church has either already been judged or will be judged very soon." In keeping with this parable of sorts, sheep who attend church regularly are those who are afraid of the outside elements of a dangerous and sinful world, ---and rightly so-- Therefore, it makes sense to run inside church walls for protection. Yet, in keeping with the symbols, when we run inside, we find that there is no light. God is light. In Him there is no darkness at all. No light--No God!!!!! So what do we do? We "make do!!!"

Since Jesus Christ of Nazareth is the Light and His people are referred to "as lights", the next logical thought is that He is not the Head of the organized church and very few of His people are attending church. So what of the massive, mega congregations? Same thing. No light. No God. i's just a crowd of gatherers worshiping someone that they refer to as Jesus. Since the path to Christ is NOT the broad but the narrow way where few be that find it, wherever the crowd gathers, there is sin crouching at the door."

In addition, there is no running water in the condemned building--- no rivers of living water---therefore, no Holy Ghost. Without the Holy Ghost, then the 7 stars are removed. The 7 stars are the of God.(Rev.1:20) Angels are assigned to the churches to guard and protect each flock. Without the Holy Ghost and the of God, it is understandable why the sheep are being spiritually damaged by the shepherds---- The RATS are the wolves in sheep's clothing---- hirelings---the so called shepherds of the flock---- countless pastors who fellowship with un-cleaness, ie. the roaches.

So it stands to reason, that if this parable be from the Lord, then the leaders of the church as it now stands have fared poorly in the Lord's eyes. If this be so, then what about the sheep? Sheep need shepherds?!!! Where are the shepherds of the Lord? A condemned building can stand, maybe for years but ultimately, the beams and the walls will crumble and fall. If it doesn't fall, then the city will come along with a bulldozer and "take it down." How will the organized church come down? Read Revelation Ch. 17 and Rev. 18 about "the harlot" called Mystery Babylon.

After the fall of the towers of the World Trade Center, we thought that Rev. Ch. 18 was fulfilled for several reasons. However, one fact caused us to know that the dust fallout in NYC and the fall of "world trade" was not the complete fulfillment of this chapter. Why? Because the World Trade Center is being rebuilt. The scripture clearly states that when Babylon falls, there will be no rebuilding of her. So we wrongly assumed that Mystery Babylon was NYC. Our founder was born and raised in NYC. Therefore, in error, Pam warned everyone she knew to "come out of her." After a few years passed, we all realized that NYC is NOT Babylon, nor is the USA. Any one who knows the Lord realizes that He would not command us to "come out of her, my people" (Rev. 18:4), "lest you share in her sins, lest you receive of her plagues," unless there was an actual place where we could flee to.

Where are God's people? Well, for the most part, God's people are known to be in the organized church. If Mystery Babylon were an actual city or nation, where on earth could all of God's people go in an exodus of unimaginable global proportions? Recognizing the signs of the time, a few Christians have already fled to Canada, believing that in doing so, they are going to escape the fall of America. In truth, America is not Babylon. God's people are everywhere so where are His people in every nation on the planet supposed to go? To the Moon or to Mars?

No. we don't know about you but we don't own a space ship. Even though several mega-tv evangelists own personal jet planes, they don't own space ships!!! Nor are we planning to book passage on Ashtar's Mothership! Regardless of what anybody says, America is the best country in the entire world. Meaning no disrespect to non-American readers, seekers of freedom from around the world flee their native lands all the time to find a safe harbor on American shores. There is no actual "place" that God's people can go to on this earth where they can find more religious freedom. The darker side is that the home of religious freedom has become a haven for Maitreya, Sananda and the rest of the fallen angaels under their command.

An additional irony is that the USA is a country founded upon the flight of spiritually oppressed people from the Old World. However, since Christopher Columbus, oppressed Americans have no earthly place that we ourselves can flee to. Think about it. Can all of God's people in the USA fit into Canada? Let's be real, here. Anyway, if America is to fall, how safe is Canada? Canada is just around the corner from us. We'd be better off in Australia or the South Pole!!!!

BUT Fear not!!! Mystery Babylon could certainly not be a physical place. We are not alone in our belief that Mystery Babylon is a metaphor symbolizing idolatrous religion. The "judged" church is not Mystery Babylon in its totality, but merely a part of it. Actually, there are several signs that the organized churches of today will eventually unite with all of the other false religions that relegate our Lord to a mere teacher or a prophet who they claim is a created being, "not divine".

Yet we anticipate that most of the true church will rise out of a righteous remnant that still remains within the organized church and others whom the Lord has touched and called who have never been church members. We also realize that the outpouring of the spirit of God upon ALL flesh is coming upon "the remnant church" but clearly, the Holy Ghost will not manifest Himself in a corrupt place. The Lord will not put new wine into old wineskins. However, where the rivers will flow, we do not yet know.

Does the "new thing" require buildings to do the work of the Lord.? No, but if so, we suspect that buildings will be used on a very limited scale. The early church of the book of Acts was not organized, as followers of the resurrected Lord assembled in each other's homes. Likewise, the "new thing" will not be an organized infrastructure with boards, bishops and buildings either!!!! The only covering required is the Head Himself, Jesus Christ of Nazareth. Praise His Holy Name!!!

Be warned that no one will be able to stand in the way of "the new thing." We have perceived some signs that quietly and secretly the Holy Ghost has been taking His time over the last few decades, preparing righteous and holy shepherds--Joshuas and Calebs--- who have been refined in the fires of trial, trouble and tribulation--- leaders across the globe. There are not many of them, but like Gideon's army, there will be enough to do the job.

So what should we do in the meantime? Well, we should watch, pray and wait. Some of God's people have already heeded the call and we have "come out of her." Others of you may have to stay within the condemned building for a time or at least on its periphery, until you too "hear the call." Only God Himself should be the One to call you out. Some people are addicted to church and if they were to "come out"prematurely, without the proper care and support systems in place, additional spiritual damage could be incurred. As withdrawal from alcohol without medical supervision is life threatening, so too, a mass exodus from the organized church at the present moment may be too shocking to the spiritual system of longterm "churchaholics."

Actually, it is wise NOT to come out until you hear the Holy Ghost for yourself. The problem is that most sheep within church walls for a considerable length of time are so deaf and so blind that they simply cannot hear and they cannot see. Moreover, the enemy has built up a formidable stronghold by seducing them to heed and believe false doctrines or to become emotionally attached to pastors, buildings, church traditions, choir members, etc.. The god of this world has blinded them, almost beyond repair. (II Cor 4:3,4) Only God Himself can release the prey of the mighty and set free the lawfully captive. (Isaiah 49:24-26) In each case of spiritual blindness, prayer should beseech the Father based upon His mercy, grace and pardon.

A WORD FROM PASTOR PAM:
Is The Organized Church An "Evil" Tree?

In my work as a deliverance counselor, I am being put into contact with too many longterm, faithful churchgoers who are practically demon possessed. Now this phenomena just did not make sense to me until I learned about the hidden, unseen influence of the fallen who call themselves "ascended masters." I believe that enough history has been presented in this book to stir our commonsense that since the tree was evil a century ago, the fruit is evil now.

One thing I have learned through the practice of deliverance, the casting out of devils, is that I really don't help anyone. Actually, I have never helped anyone!!!! It is always the Holy Spirit who does the work. Whether I lay hands or not, I am never actually DOING the work. For example, Moses was told to raise his rod over the waters and the RED SEA opened. Do you think that Moses actually opened the Red Sea with a rod? So the rod that the church is definitely not using is to "speak to the demons."

The Lord revealed to me recently that if I did not speak to the demons in a particular individual, they would not come out. However, I am really not the one casting them out. It is the Holy Spirit. I just use the Name of Jesus and stand in faith with His name. I do nothing else. I am like Moses with a rod in my hand and that rod is the power and authority of the Name of Jesus against demons.

Furthermore, I am finding from my own personal experience as a good, sincere pastor, that those who have been faithful members, followers of my ministry bare significantly less fruit than those that I counsel as a professional, Christian therapist on a weekly basis. So I had to ask myself yet another simple question. Why IS that? Someone can come into telephone counseling with me for 6 months to a year and bare ten times more spiritual fruit than some who have faithfully attended my "church" for 5 years, 10 years and even as long as 15 years. It should also be pointed out that there are people connected to my ministry that have heard countless sermons and teachings. I have known them personally and been an active figure in their lives, yet spiritual fruit in Christ is barely visible.

I believe the Holy Spirit has recently given me my answer. Don't hold on too tightly to your pew or to your pulpit. Here is the simple, yet profound answer that tells me that "church as we know it is over!." The passive model of church, where the pastor gets up on a platform, gives "a word" after the choir sings, DOES NOT BARE FRUIT. To bare real fruit for Christ, each sheep must be individually fed through counsel, guidance, up front and in your face ministry at least one hour a week, one on one.

As the babe grows, the contact can be reduced after a year or so. Once the babe is a mature Christian, then he or she can "feed his or her self and then become a worker in the church to feed new babes. One shepherd can feed about 4 sheep a day, 7 days a week, for about 6 months to a year or about 27 people at a time. If the sheep learn quickly, then this would be about 54 babes a year. As a writer and a trainer, I cannot do a full time job of counseling sheep. Full time pastoring would consists of 6- 8 sheep a a day for six months or a year.

Consider a case in point. A young woman came to Jesus by way of a Mormon outreach and the Blue Book, as she watched Christian television. She truly was convinced that she was saved by repeating a sinner's prayer, yet almost immediately, demons began to imitate the

Holy Ghost. This client was sent by a supernatural experience to the ministry of a mega preacher whose name I cannot mention to protect the client's confidentiality. This client gave up fornication, and became a very faithful church member, Yet as time when on, the demons became more active.

So she sat in church, sought counsel from her pastor, who referred her to another pastor. Ultimately, this client found me through the Internet that The Lord sent her to me primarily to expose the problem. The Holy Spirit revealed to me that if I don't speak to that demon, it will NOT come out. I have spoken to it and it has laughed and giggled back at me. But I am convinced that it WILL come out but unfortunately the client did not proceed because she was just "too churched." Even so, she is truly blessed because I have done the most difficult task of all.

Try to imagine how hard it is for someone who looks saved, acts saved, sounds saved, goes to bible study not once but twice a week and twice on Sunday, does not drink, fornicate, and tithes too?!!!! Beloved readers, that is practically impossible. On top of that, she is in the ministry of a mega preacher, no less!!!!! I have been looked down upon by clients who merely study the works of mega preachers, much less who are in their company on a regular basis.

Yet, I was able to prove and convince this client that she could not possibly be saved because she has been worshiping the fake Jesus, Sananda Immanuel, an un-resurrected, impostor---a fallen angel. If I don't do anything else, I have done my job. This particular client did not understand either repentance or resurrection, and so it was very obvious to me from the beginning, in spite of all of her good works, that she was not saved. In truth, I have accomplished a major task with this young woman. For several others have hung up the phone on me with a "how dare you question my salvation."

If it were not for the torment and the fact that this young woman is hungry for the truth, she would be just another statistic of a person who "missed it" for reasons that are not of her own doing. I commend her because even some professing Christians who are seriously demon oppressed have refused my counsel, blind and foolish are they. Yet, where I really throw my hands up in the air is not over this one person. It is over the countless millions who are in the same boat as this young woman, either sitting in a church somewhere, or God help them, learning on their own from Christian television.

For example, droves of people are responding to the call in various mega churches and taken into another room to receive the gift of tongues. The issue here is not that mega preachers don't preach Christ. They do!!!! Nevertheless, I learned something from my caseload that I did not realize before. I only recently discovered that the fake Jesus uses a twisted interpretation of word of God to birth disciples into his own kingdom. Well, he DOES!!!!

Most astounding is that in practically ALL of my cases of demonic torment, a common factor is that 95 percent of them were not demon possessed BEFORE THEY WENT TO CHURCH!!!!. It is one thing to come to church and miss it. It is yet another to listen to someone who claims to know Christ preach and then pick up a powerful religious demon that is extremely difficult to get rid of. Yet there is a simple formula to overcome the Sananda/Maitreya influence. Churchgoers need to go back to ground zero and be convicted of sin through the spirit of repentance. They need to be brought back to the cross. They clearly do not understand resurrection nor repentance. The job of revolutionaries like myself is to rightly divided the word to them on both of those subjects. Whether the Lord delivers them of the religious demon first and then immediately saves them or the reverse, is clearly up to Him. In prayer, the task is to come boldly before the throne of grace and seek God's mercy, since many churchgoers are not at fault here.

IT IS THE FAULT OF THE ORGANIZED CHURCH!!!!!

The reason why I did a double take, threw my hands up in the air and put my pastorate on the altar of God is because I finally realized that the models that are out there are for the most part, ARE NOT WORKING, in spite of the billions of dollars that are being spent on "preaching a gospel" which apparently is not THE-EEEEE gospel. From my personal background and experience, I could clearly see that the denominations were not working and I have grown to a place where I know that unless there is wide-scale repentance within the denominational church, they are coming DOWN!!! Yet, the gruesome fact is that the day for repentance may have already passed!

I have known for a while now that the Fake Jesus has been using the non-denominations and Christian cults like the Mormons, but I certainly did not fathom the extent of the problem. Whether it be denominations, non-denominations, Christian television or radio, I finally came to terms with the fact that those who believe that they have done the right things yet they have gotten the wrong results is a clear sign that NONE OF IT IS WORKING!!!!!

Several of my clients have done wrong things--- sins of all kinds, witchcraft, incest, you name it but some of my clients have done absolutely no wrong to be subjected to the kind of demonic torment that they endure every hour of the day. In fact, they have lived lives that Christians who are not being tormented by demons should emulate. It is sad to say but there are countless faithful church goers who have been out and out deceived by religion and religious people. I can find no excuse to place the blame on the deceived.

Today, people are being saved and delivered, one at a time over the telephone through the work of the Deliverance Counseling Center. We are available 7 days a week, 16 hours a day. Yet once the Lord opened our eyes to the deceptive work of the ascended masters, we too had to adjust and be prepared for change. In truth, the model that we have ALL been using---bringing huge crowds as well as small groups into small and big barn---, on a "believe and receive" gospel devoid of the godly sorrow of repentance is a ministry of the Fake Jesus.

Let's face it and be real here. As a denominational pastor for years, I myself could do absolutely nothing. Yet today, the tide is turning, the Holy Spirit is moving and people are being saved and delivered. My job is very simple. I preach the gospel of repentance and the bodily resurrection of the Lord and the Holy Spirit is moving on hardened hearts to lead people to repent, giving them the faith to believe on Jesus. I am casting out demons---on the telephone, no less--- from those who will humble themselves to receive it.

This one referenced case has taught me that since the organized church is not working, radio and tv is not working, it would be useless for me to reinvent the wheel cause it wouldn't work with me either. It hasn't and it won't. I don't know any other models other than working with people one on one. I have been out on the street in street ministry. That DOES work if the basic gospel is being preached and the street evangelist is not bringing people into a church that is going to confuse them.

What I am expecting is that the Lord is going to do a mass thing, around the world, similar to what He did to me and for me. I was an atheist and I was not seeking Him. He came after me in a dream and brought me to the cross without the benefit of man. I was sent to church, not to be nurtured, but that I would understand and perceive the problem and learn what NOT to do about 25 years later. More than two decades of "Church" has not done much for me. As I wrote in the "Making of a Prophet: A Spiritual Indictment to the Organized Church", I have remained a root in dry ground.

I got a hunger for the word from Kenneth Copeland and others and Joyce Meyer provided some good, solid teaching. But for the most part, I was attracted to Copeland and the rest of them because they were "supernatural" and my background was in witchcraft. The occult and the charismatic movement are almost an extension of each other and so I found word of faith to be "comfortable"---in other words, charismatic witchcraft. The denominations harmed me in the beginning because they were loose on sin and so until I got grounded on my own and took dominion over my own sin, I fell to carnal ministers. But once I had sexual sin under control, the denominations did not really harm me. They may have hurt my feelings and injured my pride, but they didn't harm me. They couldn't harm me because I was saved BEFORE I arrived. Just as the denomination I was in didn't know the truth, I didn't know the truth either. We were differently yet equally ignorant.

My major point is that the church as it is now operating today is "doing harm" to people who are serious about finding Jesus. And I shudder at the thought. I KNOW the problem. The problem has already been laid out in other chapters through the presentation of an historical perspective. I thought I KNEW the organizational solution. Once, I thought that the answer was in home fellowships, in spite of the many problems that can affect that also. You see, I really didn't realize just how much the devil has penetrated the church. I have faith that God is going to do something. I am simply throwing up my hands and praying, "Lord, this battle is YOURS and I don't have a clue as to how you plan to deal with it. Just "cause me to be ready."

Once I said this prayer just a year ago, I was shown that I have not really been "a root in dry ground." I too have been contaminated by the beliefs, traditions and practices of both the denominational and the non-denominational Protestant church. It seems that every week, the Lord brings to my attention some practice or some area of biblical "mis-" interpretation that I need to be cleansed from. On Wednesday, June 25, 2008, I was put to the test. I passed it but I can't say that it was easy.

To make a long and involved story short, four years ago, my enemies within the denomination where I served from 1979-2004 found a not so legitimate excuse to put me off of the church rolls. In other words, I was ex-communicated or dis-fellowshipped for $660. Those who try to minimize the truth that I bring often accuse me of unforgiveness and bitterness against the church at large because I was spiritually abused. Not so. Not so at all. The truth is that I knew 9 months before I was actually ousted that God Himself desired that I come out of the church. To learn more about my testimony, I suggest that you obtain "the Making of A Prophet." On the Wednesday in question, I showed up at the annual meeting which was held just 15 minutes from my home. I was certainly led to go, but I was not sure as to the reason.

    I had planned to arrive at the business meeting, to greet everyone, share about the 4 books that I have written in 4 years, and then make my farewells. However, I walked into the church doors while one of my former ministerial peers was preaching and the communion table was set, so I sat down on a back pew. Immediately, the sermon began to grip me in my spirit, preaching right down my alley so to speak. It was like I had never left. I did my usual cadence in support of the preacher---amen, hallelujah, thank you, Jesus, and so on. Heads started to turn at the sound of a familiar voice and people started smiling as they fluttered their fingers at me in greeting. Then, it happened. The Bishop gave the invitation by declaring that the doors of the church were opened. A strong compulsion came over me to walk down that aisle and I felt like invisible hands were nudging me in my back.

    I knew that if I were to do so, my walk down the aisle would be a false sign to the church body that I was coming back to them, yet I got up from the pew and went forward just the same to the sounds of various people greeting me as if I was the returning prodigal daughter. When I arrived at the altar, the ministerial leadership inquired, "are you to returning to re-establish your ministry?" Quietly, I informed them out of the hearing of the congregation that my walk down the aisle was merely a demonstration of my reconciliation with them, and that I harbored no unforgiveness. I was treated as a friendly visitor, allowed to speak and greet the congregation and I did so, graciously. On a break, I heard words from a bishop's mouth that I had once longed to hear, which went something like this. "Reverend, anything you want from me, all you have to do is ask, and its done!"

It was a lovely day of fellowship, but a few days later, I heard from the Lord. What He revealed was a tough pill to swallow, but I did so without regret, tears, or frustration. I will try to express in words the the thoughts that filled my mind:

> "Pam, the delicious, emotional and sensual feeling that attempted to overtake you in June 2008 is the very same feeling that you did not resist in 1979. That same feeling caused you to join this very same church. In fact, I called you out 4 years later in 1983 when you heard my audible voice say to you, "Come Out! Separate." However, you rejoined when you returned to the church for a funeral in 1987, thinking that the delicious feeling you once again experienced was from Me.
>
> As it was not from Me in 1979. It was not from Me in 1987. And it was NOT from Me in 2008. I never sent you to that church not ONE time but I allowed the fake Jesus to deceive you so that you would learn that those who are really ANOINTED by me hear from Me "without a feeling." You did not rejoin this time because YOU know that you will not find Me there. You have passed the test."

> Is the passing of this test indicative of my readiness for God's new thing? Perhaps. If not, then I am close. Of one thing, I am assured. The truth is unrolling itself like a scroll before the eyes of those who are willing to be chastened by God. In the meantime, I intend to continue to preach righteousness and truth, both by mouth and on the printed page. The Lord does His work of deliverance, and from time to time, allows me to share in His power. I am committed to testing everything I receive in the spirit and then writing the truth as I become aware of it.

As we become willing to examine EVERYTHING we have been taught or practiced within the organized church, the Holy Ghost will open our spiritual ears to hear, to understand and to obey Him when He calls our name out of Mystery Babylon. By His grace and mercy, we pray for you--- that He will restore your spiritual hearing and your spiritual sight, as long as the condition of your heart is sincere, meek and upright. You yourself have an unction from God to see and if you hunger and thirst after righteousness, when the time is right, you will hear His call.

So where should you attend church while you "watch and wait" for the Lord's "new thing?" Good question. Everyone is not like us. As a watchman, Pam was actually called to stand without affiliation with the organized church on any level. Some of you may have a different calling. Her advice may be of some value to you, as it is based upon decades of experience with the denominational and the non-denominational, charismatic word of faith movement:

> In truth, I personally believe that the best option---the wisest choice--is to

stay out of the organized church entirely, especially if you are a babe in Christ or one who is lost, but seeking Him. I am not a babe yet, I did not immediately recognize that the power that came on me recently was a counterfeit until a few days later. The people assembled were not to blame for they are totally ignorant of the invisible forces who are behind everything they say and do. Though short, Satan is now enjoying his hour by the seat that has been established for him through the work of fallen angels. However, if you are a churchgoer and you are still attached or even addicted to "church",
then know this. By far, if you are attending a charismatic church, be it pentecostal, or word of faith, you are not in a safe place. In spite of its deadness and widespread sin from the pulpit to the pew, the better of two very bad choices is the denominational church.

So Be safe, God's People!

BIBLIOGRAPHY
of Internet Articles

Chapter Two

Title: John Todd, The Illuminati and Witchcraft
www.kt70/~jamesjpn/article/john_tod_and_the_illuminati.htm

Title: Something Wicked This Way Comes or Helter Skelter, Run For Shelter
Author: Whisler, James
URL://poweredbychrist.homestead.com/something_weicked_2.html

Title: The Illuminati and the Council on Foreign Relations
URL:www.biblebelievers.org.au/illuminati.htm

Title: The Great White Brotherhood
Wikipedia Free Encyclopedia
URL://en.wikipedia.org/wiki/Great_White_Brotherhood

Chapter Three

Title: About the Late Sister Thedra
URL: www.wolflodge.org/sananda/sister_thedra.htm

Title: The United Forces of Light: "Messages from Sananda"
URL:
http://piazza.cal.n/users/lightnet/celestial/forceoflightHYPERLINK
"http://piazza.cal.n/users/lightnet/celestial/forceoflightmessages.htm"
messages.htm

Title: George King (Aetherius Society)
The Wikipedia Free Encyclopedia
URL: http://en.wikipedia.org/wiki/george_j_king

Title: Alice Bailey
The Wikipedia Free Encyclopedia
URL: http://en.wikipedia.org/wiki/Alice_Bailey

Title: Alice Bailey: The Plan
LET US REASON TOGETHER
URL: www.letusreason.org/NAM20.htm

Title: Benjamin Crème, Maitreya, the Ascended Masters and Lucifer
Author: Melanson, Terry
URL:
www.conspiracyarchive.com/NewAge/Creme_ HYPERLINK "http://www.conspiracyarchive.com/NewAge/Creme_Maitreya.htm" Maitreya.htm

Title: Angels: Servants of God or New Age Messengers?
URL: http://temaa1p315.homestead.com/new_age_.html

Chapter Four

Title: Walk-Ins
Url: www.crystalinks.com/walk_ins.html

Title: Walk-Ins, Wanderers and Light Workers
URL: www.angelicinspirations.com/page188.htm

Title: Walk-Ins Now Here To Move Us Into New World Order
URL: www.cuttingedge.org/NEWS/n1286.cfm

Title: How to Buid a Golden Age
URL/www.saintgermainfreedom.com/K_GASOCIETY/SPIRITUALRAYS/AASpiritualraysmain.html"http://www.saintgermainfreedom.com/K_GASOCIETY/HYPERLINK " www.saintgermainfreedom.com/K_GASOCIETY/SPIRITUALRAYS/AASpiritualraysmain.html"SPIRITUALRAYS/AASpiritualraysmain.html

Title: Saint Germain's Strategy for the Golden Age
URL:www.lightparty.com/HYPERLINK www.lightparty.com/Spirituality/StGermainsStrategy.html" Spirituality/StGermainsStrategy.html

Title: Are Christians Supposed to Take Dominion?
Author:Bowman,Robert
URL://iclnet.org/pub/resources/text/cri/crijrnl/web/crj0024a.html

Chapter Five

Title: Christian Yoga
ACF Newsource: The Osgood File (CBS Radio Network, 8/18/03
URL:www.acfnewsource.org/religion/christian_yoga.htm

Title: Can Yoga Be Christian?
A Chapter from "Yoga, A Path to God."
Author: Hughes, Louis
URL:www.bodymindmeditation.ie/yoga.htm

Chapter Seven

Title: "The Truth About Roman Catholicism"
Author: Reynolds, M.H.
URL:
"../../../../the_truth_about_catholicism.html"//catholic.cephasministry.com/the_truth_about_catholicism.html)

Title: History of Divine Healing
URL:
www.hendrickson.com/pdf/chapters/1565637143.ch_o1.pdf
Title: Tongues, The Bible Evidence:
The Revival Legacy of Charles F. Parham
Author: McGee, Gary B.

URL: //enrichmentjournal.ag.org/199903/068_tongues.cfm
Title: A Wolf In Sheep's Clothing: "How Charles Finney's Theology Ravaged the Evangelical Movement
Author: Johnson, Phillip R.

URL: www.spurgeon.org/~phil/articles/finney.htm

Title: Speaking in Tongues in the Mormon Churches
Brean Christian Ministries
URL: www.frontiernet/~bcmmin/tongue/.htm

Title: Speaking in Tongues: An Un-Sound Evidence of Salvation
Author: Greer, Nick
URL:

Title: Marie Woodworth-Etter: Signs and Wonders
URL: www.lit4ever.org/questions.html

Title: History of Christianity
Wikipedia Free Encyclopedia
URL: en.wikipedia.org

History of Early Christianity (33-325)

Church of the Roman Empire (313-476)
Church of the Early Middle Ages (476-800)
Church of the High Middle Ages (800-1499)
Church Age of Discovery (1492-1769)
Church and the enlightenment(1580-1800)
Contemporary Church History (1848-present)

Title: Church Leaders (1800-present)
Wikipedia Free Encyclopedia
URL: en.wikipedia.org/wiki/

Joseph Smith/ Joseph_Smith
Mother Ann Lee/Ann_Lee
John Alexander Dowie/John_Alexander_Dowie
Charles Parham/Charles_Parham
William Seymour/William_J._Seymour
Charles Finney /Charles_Finney
Marie Woodworth-Etter/Marie_Woodworth-Etter
Evan Roberts/Evan_Roberts(minister)
Jessie Penn-Lewis/Jessie_Penn-Lewis
George King/George_King
Alice Bailey/Alice_Bailey
Helen Blavatsky/Helen_Blavatsky
Oral Roberts/Oral_Roberts
Kathryn Khulman/Kathryn_Khulman
Benny Hinn/Benny_Hinn

APPENDIX

FINDING A CHURCH IN THESE TIMES

Many readers and visitors to our websites at bewarechristian.com and deliverancecounseling.com will be shocked to hear a minister of 26 years write that for most of you, it is best that you not attend church in your local community. I have a pastor's heart and have functioned in the pastor's calling for about 15 of those years, and I am still a pastor. However, I personally believe that a person can grow spiritually without regularly attending an organized church.

Most definitely, you should assemble with the saints, but the word of God does not lay out a detailed order of service, nor does it suggest the day you should assemble, the time or even the nature of the place or building where gathering together should take place. We live in a computerized world, where we can "assemble" 24 and 7. Simply put, I truly believe that the organized church as it now stands will be completely revamped by the Lord. Why? Because quite frankly, the traditional structures are not working. I myself have no replacements to offer, as Healing Waters is in the process of being completely revamped and reformed.

When I wrote the first 3 books, I was hopeful that repentance would bring about reformation and renewal to the organized church. However, the love of money, which is the root of ALL evil, has permeated most of the church and I seriously doubt if the Lord is going to allow it to continue to exist in its present state. Judgment is swiftly coming and I shunder at what is going to happen to church and to churchgoers. In the meantime, for those of you who feel that you need to assemble in an organized church, the following additional comments are provided for you to assist you in your pursuit to find a church. The following excerpt is taken from various passages in "Faces of the

Religious Demon" and "The Making of a Prophet."

In truth, I do not believe that Jesus intended for any one who follows Him to lower their spiritual guard by relying on others to watch on his behalf. Just as we don't need a weather man to tell us that spring is coming, we also don't need people to complicate the obvious. Case in point. If the Anti-Christ is actually a human being, then it is clear to me that he shall come forth out of Christianity for a very simple reason. Satan has had a seat in the organized church for centuries. There is no better place for the devil to conceal, prepare and empower his son of evil and destruction than within a worldly Christian system.

The word of God clearly testifies not only to the fact that demons were operating during the Lord's earthly ministry, but that renewed demonic activity will manifest in the latter days. (I Timothy Ch:4:1-4) Paul's warning to Timothy does not merely relate to new manifestations of evil in the world but to an ever increasing apostasy in the professing church, a cult promoted by seducing spirits of a highly sensitive spirituality. In spite of this infiltration by demons into the organized church, it is not my personal intent to disparage the local church or to suggest that all local churches need to be closed down. I myself pastor a local assembly as well as an international Internet body of believers. However, the organized church is an institution created by man, not even described or promoted by the Word of God:

"There is nothing inherently wrong with being involved in a local church. But realize that being part of a group that calls itself a "church" does not make you saved, holy, righteous, or godly any more than being in Yankee Stadium makes you a professional baseball player. Participating in church-based activities does not necessarily draw you closer to God or prepare you for a life that satisfies Him or enhances your existence....Sadly, many people will label this view 'blasphemy.'. However, you should realize that the Bible neither describes nor promotes the local church as we know it today. Many centuries ago religious leaders created the prevalent form of 'church' that is so widespread in our society to help people be better followers of Christ. But the local church many have come to cherish---the services, offices, programs, buildings, ceremonies---is neither biblical nor un-biblical. It is a-biblical--- that is, such an organization is not addressed in the Bible." (Revolution, pg. 37) 5

Therefore, since the church model of modern times is neither promoted nor discredited in the Word of God, I believe that it's viability should be determined by some very wise and practical applications:

1. In terms of its structure, is it an episcopal denomination or an independent body? Quite frankly, if it is a connected church, then even

though it may be uncorrupted at the local level, linked to an ungodly authority or "Mother Church" will eventually spoil or damage the spiritual fruits throughout the entire system. By nature of its organization, a religious demon will have a seat in high places. The complicated, political form of an episcopal church with a connected governing body should be avoided primarily due to its structure. Consequently, its bishops and leaders will be prone to cover-ups, particularly where improprieties and outright sin may be involved among its various charges. In my second book, I describe this dilemma:

"A Bishop's power lies in his ability to appoint a pastor and fill a pulpit. Since pastors in full time ministry are totally dependent each year upon whether or not the Bishop chooses to favor them with an appointment to a church that will be lucrative enough to continue to provide for themselves and their families, a conflict of interest automatically inherent within the Episcopal form of church government will ultimately manifest." (The Making of A Prophet, pg. 84) 6

Dealing with sin in such a structure is like trying to eliminate roaches from a city block where all of the buildings are erected side by side and are therefore "connected". If you bomb one apartment with a pesticide, or even exterminate an entire building, the roaches will simply run upstairs, downstairs or to the building next door. Regardless of how clean you keep your apartment, you will not be able to contain the roaches, especially after dark. Just go in the kitchen and turn on your lights and hundreds of them will be flying around as if they had wings!!! Every connected building has to be bombed from one corner to the other on the entire street, or the roaches will soon return. So is the fate of the connected churches. The leaven of the Pharisees is impossible to contain without a complete annihilation.

2. Where an independent church is concerned, the issue is not so much its structure but whether or not it has a system in place to avoid spiritual neglect or abuse. Within a small assembly or a mega church, every sheep in that church should have someone who personally knows him and who ministers to his personal needs. If members are compelled to go outside of their local church to receive competent counseling, deliverance, healing and recovery, then I suspect that the primary benefit experienced in church is merely a soothing of their flesh as as a by-product of the worship experience of song and praise. Moreover, congregations of this kind provide a social environment for family members. In my opinion, social contacts with Christians can be obtained at a Christian concert and family activities are available at the local YMCA. If your spiritual needs are not being met at your local church, then you are just involved in a social club and your local church has no real spiritual value. Recently I learned that state of the art children's ministry programs can become traps

due to the fact that the parents won't leave a church even when they realize that the basic core of the church is corrupt. The pressures for disatisfied parents to remain are exerted by the social and entertainment needs of their children.

3. The independent churches that can be very dangerous include those that call themselves "deliverance churches." In some of these assemblies, the religious demon and the witchcraft spirit are running rampant with counterfeits in worship, doctrine, prayer and other strange practices including a heavy emphasis on being slain in the spirit.

"A demonstration of real power is not falling slain. We see a lot of this phenomena in the ministries of TV evangelists, particularly in the Pentecostal and non-denominational churches. Demonstration of God's power would be after you have fallen out in the spirit, what condition were you in when you got to your feet?!!! Where you healed? Were you delivered? Did God speak to you a word in due season concerning a special problem you have been challenged with? Or did you just pass out because everybody else was passing out!? (The Making of a Prophet, pg. 199) 7

4. I agree with Dr. Rebecca Brown's warning concerning various counterfeits manifested through the speaking in other tongues, primarily among word of faith, pentecostal and Charismatic Catholic churches:

"Christians have made the terrible mistake of assuming that ALL tongues are from God. How wrong they are!...It is well known that many occultic rituals are done in tongues....The fact that Catholics speak in tongues is not proof that they are filled with the Holy Spirit. Too many of these precious Catholic souls assume that because they are speaking in tongues, they are saved. How can the Holy Spirit be operative and manifesting in a system of idolatry? Those involved in the Catholic Charismatic movement who really start reading and studying the Bible soon realize they must separate themselves from the idolatrous Roman Catholic Church if they are going to serve the true Jesus of the Bible." (Prepare for War, pgs. 182,183) 8

5.However, the crucial factors of your assessment of a local church actually relate to the security of your eternal life,which is truly where the rubber meets the road. Why go to church if, in the final analysis, you do not escape damnation by traveling the narrow way to eternal life? Assuredly, you should examine how and with what regularity the doctrines of repentance, resurrection and rebirth are being preached and taught? A church with a Jezebel influence will minimize or overlook the importance of these "3 R's" through excessive tradition, polity and other less important priorities of doctrine.

6.If a local church minimizes the need to learn the devices of the devil or does not even recognize the existence and the workings of demonic forces in these times, then it is in a low condition of spiritual life and power. I believe that such a church should be avoided like the plague. In fact, such ignorance on the part of a congregation's leadership is an indication to demons of the leaders' accommodation to them through fear, an open door to demonic influence. According to Jessie Penn-Lewis:

"A perspective view of the ages covered by the history in Bible records, shows that the rise and fall in spiritual power of the people of God, was marked by the recognition of the existence of the demoniacal host of evil. When the Church of God in the old and new dispensations was at the highest point of spiritual power, the leaders recognized, and drastically dealt with, the invisible forces of Satan and when at the lowest, they were ignored, or allowed to have free course, among the people." (War on the Saints, 9th edition, pg.27)

Consequently, if there is no emphasis in the local church on spiritual warfare and deliverance, that church is without spiritual power.

7. The emphasis upon the Word of God in a church should and could be a good sign; Nevertheless, it is misleading and immaterial to base your assessment of a church solely upon evidence that all its members carry bibles, yellow markers and recite scriptures. For when leadership doe not rightly divide the word, then heresies posing as revelation truths give place to

the doctrines of devils that Paul warned Timothy about (I Timothy 4:1): the prosperity gospel, dominion teaching, "name it and claim it", pre-tribulation rapture, submission to authority, eternal security, no ordination for women, and other doctrines too numerous to mention even in one book.

False doctrines of this kind are skillfully birthed by teaching demons to deceive and exploit the people. If the devil had nerve enough to get "religious" by reciting scripture out of its context to tempt the Lord Jesus Himself, then he has trained his demonic army to do likewise to us. (Matthew 4:1-11) "Out of context" preaching tends to draw those who have not truly repented nor been converted, but who are enticed to come to church by the excitement that scriptural hype can produce. Such preaching and teaching draws people, places and things to the building.---those who seek blessings to get their needs met or to fulfill their dreams---but they have not really been drawn to Christ.

8. A church after the Lord's heart is the church of Philadelphia: those who do not deny His name and who have kept His word.(Revelation 3:7-13) This is a church that will not compromise the truth, either for the favor of the world or for unity with other churches. Since we all see through a glass darkly, a good pastor is one who continually examines if he is rightly dividing the word. <u>When errors and contradictions are uncovered, then a good pastor openly and</u>

<u>publicly admits to his or her mistakes, correcting any inaccurate teachings without hesitation.</u> The Lord declared that the church of Philadelphia was of little strength, so it is clear that His assessment was not based upon numbers of members, wealth or resources. I believe that a major part of keeping His word is to go forth and cast out demons. A good church is about building people so that they can confront the demonic influences to expel the darkness in their own environment, equipping the sheep to be living stones, holy vessels for the Spirit of the Lord to dwell in.

THE DIARY OF A PASTOR: CHURCH IS NOT WORKING!

Christian television would work if it repeated the same message of salvation over and over again. People would be able to be saved in their living room. Then if they went to church, at least their salvation would be assured, in spite of any error they might be taught. However, preaching a salvation message every day would not work "in the world's system of media communication" because ratings are based upon diversity. This is why the mega TV preachers are prone to add to or take away from the pure and simple gospel. Jesus crucified, buried and raised doesn't play well for either television or radio.

All babes in Christ need someone to feed them the word of God. They need to be able to ask personalized questions and receive answers relevant and specific to their needs. Even a Christian talk show can be deceiving because people who are untrained and unskilled in the word of God will take the advice they hear sent to a particular caller, and improperly apply it to their own particular situation. After I was saved and still a babe in Christ, I fed myself off of the tapes of Kenneth Copeland, Kenneth Hagin, Fred Price and several others. I pumped one tape after another into my head. I misapplied the scriptures on faith to some real life situations where if I had had a personal teacher, I could have learned a lot quicker and avoided the pitfalls. Instead, I took what these preachers taught out of context, and wrongfully applied their teaching to my own life.

Every one needs an elder who can answer questions. As clear as I myself try to make things when I bring forth the word, invariably, someone misreads or misinterprets my teachings, even now. To counteract this problem, anyone who wants to contact me by email or by phone to ask me a question about something that I taught can do so. I answer each and every question.

Christian churches of today would work if they took the advice that Jesus gave to the 7 churches of 2000 years ago. It was one word. REPENT!!!! The problem is that they won't. Sardis didn't heed the warning. Nor Ephesus or any of the rest of them. And guess what!? Those original churches no longer exist. I would have to search out what happened to the church that the Lord commended called Philadelphia. But all of the rest of those churches are nothing but rubble and broken peices of stone, toppled by earthquakes.

NO MORE "CHUCH AS USUAL " AT OUR LOCAL ASSEMBLY

I pastored 2 AME Zion Churches in New York State. I also served for several years as an associate minister in my home church in Albany New York. From my 22 years of ministry within a denomination, I must attest to the fact that the damage had been done many years by generations before my time. Therefore, sin is now so intrinsic that it is almost impossible for denominational churches to repent. I may not have had the kind of revelation that I have now, but for the most part, I did not preach error and I was walking in the righteousness that I knew at the time. Overall, I preached a message of repentance and power.

It didn't matter. The people, both minister and laity refused to hear. So I started an independent church called "Healing Waters Christian Center" in 1996 while still in the denomination.. A year and a half ago, I realized that the "church" model was not working at Healing Waters either. So I revamped it.. For example, no more do I do a passive bible study where I do all the work and lecturing and the people just sit there in front of me. I used to do four bible studies a week, two in the morning and two at night. No more. Everyone who wants bible study must do an independent study based upon the message that they heard on Sunday. They prepare what they have learned for me, either in writing or by telephone, rather than the other way around. They also prepare questions based upon what they did not understand in the teaching. I hold these bible studies in conference calls over the telephone. Individual counseling sessions are available for all those who need it.

The service itself is also "different." It is more like an AA meeting than a traditional church worship service. However, the emphasis is the word---at least an hour. After the word is a question and answer period, a time of testimony and prayer. I rarely do public deliverances but if the spirit leads, demons could get cast out after the children have left the service. We don't over emphasize singing anymore. We may or may not sing a song or two. We leave it up to people to listen to worship music in their private devotions. Little emphasis on the offering. We leave it up to the member to send their offering over the web.

No one leaves our gathering or "meeting" with their problem unless they want to. Sometimes after the word has gone forth, all of our attention will go toward getting one person delivered in a particular area. We do not insist that people come to our gathering every time the doors are open. We direct them to the website. If the unsaved come in looking for truth, they leave "saved."No more "dress up" for Sunday. I wear jogging suits, fashionable of course, loll. No more churchy clothes unless a person wants to. Everyone is "comfortable" in whatever they want to wear. I will not tolerate people coming to church out of form and fashion.

I asked one young man who has been coming to church because of his girlfriend, "why are you here." He said "I don't know." I said "well, til you know, don't come back." One of my other regular visitors thought "Oh, that is awful. How can a pastor tell someone NOT to come to church" She herself has not been back since I said that. My motive was this. If visitors do not know that those who come to church are searching for Jesus, then they will just sit in my congregation , and become more and more confused. Visitors who do not understand who Jesus is will be in even a worst state than they were in BEFORE they came to church. They may even pick up a religious demon due to becoming habituated to church attendance, a form of godliness that denies the power thereof.

As I write this, it is January 1, 2007. These changes in the way we assemble were made on Sept 11, 2005. The Lord revealed in 2006---- that our church was not really built upon a clean foundation in 1996 because I was with a secret sin at the time, with the man who became my 3rd husband shortly after the church was founded. Even though I got married, the ministry was still "unclean." In fact, the Lord revealed that my husband was sent by the devil to infiltrate my ministry from the ground up. I believed that it was Satan's intention to spoil the work before it even got started. That was the trick. The double counterfeit. Attack the pastor unmercifully so that she will believe that the work she is doing is "highly anointed" and she won't "let it go."

It almost worked because I was deceived into believing that the Lord was in this. He wasn't. Cool. No problem. Better to know now than never. Don't get me wrong. God was in control and knew that I needed to " go through" -so that I could help others similarly deceived. The goal was to know the truth. Now that I know the truth, I thank God everyday for not allowing me to become a successful pastor of a large church or a mega preacher. I thank the Lord that He would not grow my ministry Himself while I was unclean and He would not allow the devil to grow it either. Now that the devil is out of my local assembly, I will see where the Lord takes me and Healing Waters in 2007.

July 8, 2007 I was shown that those who assemble with us have been living two lives: a Christian face before me when we assemble and a worldly face at home, on the job and in the local community. I have shut it down as of July 8th.

October 25, 2007 Wow. I learned that the religious demon that I wrote about has a name: Jesus Sananda Immanuel and Maitreya. The name of my ministry, "Healing Waters" is a Maitreya byword and has been since the early 80's when Benjamin Crème gave credit to Maitreya for "healing waters" in Mexico, where it is reported that several have been healed of cancer. I received the name through a prophecy sent to me in the mouth of an 9 year old girl on 1/8/83. After 26 years, I MUST change my ministerial name. On the web, we will now be called "bewarechristian.com." Our local fellowship will choose its own name.

DOES JESUS KNOW YOU?

A terribly shocking thing is happening in ALL the churches today. There are sincere people believing in a counterfeit Jesus, an imposter. They worship the imposter because He has some wonderful traits. He died for their sins. He is loving, sacrificial, he heals, even casts out demons it would seem, yet this Jesus is missing one crucial thing that makes him an imposter. He is not resurrected.

He is not resurrected for several reasons. Some of his followers think they know what it means "to be raised from the dead" or other expressions like "he is risen," the tomb is empty" even "Jesus is alive" but they really do not understand the truth about the doctrine of resurrection. When you directly ask them, "Is Jesus right now in a physical body, they will say "No! Jesus is now in spirit form" When asked to define resurrection, they will answer, resurrection is renewal, an end of the past and a new beginning.

Then when the Lord's bodily resurrection is explained and it is also pointed out that those who die in Jesus shall receive bodies when the Lord returns to raise them, they'll casually reply "oh, I KNEW that." Well, out of the abundance of the heart the mouth speaks. The only way anyone can confess that Jesus is raised is one who understood in his or her heart exactly what resurrection is. And if you didn't "know it" before it was explained, then you are not saved.

Some believers on the "impostor" Jesus are extremely sincere in their faith. Nevertheless, without a belief on the bodily resurrection of Jesus, then their faith is vain, and as Paul wrote to the Corinthians, "they are still in their sins." If they are still in their sins, then they are not saved. They have anchored their faith into "another Jesus", a counterfeit---an impostor---a religious demon---the spirit of the Anti-Christ.

And whose fault is this? It is not the fault of the sincere believer. It is the fault of the organized church who allowed a religious demon to enter and deceive. The organized church has not been preaching the bodily resurrection of the Lord Jesus Christ. They have preached that "Jesus went into hell and got the keys" but the organized church has NOT seen to it that those they feed the word of God UNDERSTAND the resurrection. For example, there are believers who are speaking in tongues, even casting out demons, yet they haven't a clue as to the foundational truth of the bodily resurrection of Jesus Christ. They are on fire for the impostor. The tongues they speak was not inspired by the Holy Ghost. The demons that they believe they ae casting out are laughing at them because they have a form of godliness that denies the power of the resurrection.

So if you are a faithful churchgoer and in truth, there is no spiritual fruit manifesting in your Christian walk, a lack of fruit is a clear sign that Jesus doesn't know you because in His own words, we are known by our fruits. You are probably one who "fakes it to make it." You really don't understand why the joy of the Lord has not been your strength. You are not living in peace as you are usually stressed out and/or depressed so you have no concept of the Lord's joy. Your church attendance is merely a habit and all of your Christian labor, including your tithing, your church attandance, your witnessing is all in vain. You don't really understand what is missing. It could be that you understood repentance, the cross and redemption but you didn't understand resurrection.

THE SINNER'S PRAYER

Since I wrote the book "The Making of a Prophet," the Lord has revealed to me that the sins of corrupt preachers are merely the tip of the iceberg where the problems of the organized church are concerned. Actually, the worst problem of them all has nothing at all to do with sin. It has to do with how the gospel is presented.

The organized church has misled seekers of Christ to believe that "they must accept Jesus into their lives." Simply put, the unsaved are told that they must make a decision for Christ. Consequently, countless churchgoers believe that they became saved by either getting up out of their seats on a pew and walking forward to shake a preacher's hand to receive the right hand of fellowship. Others have been led either in or out of church to repeat something known as "the sinner's prayer."

As a result, sincere people have been deceived into believing that they can "speak" themselves into salvation by a misinterpretation of the verse, "confess the Lord Jesus with your mouth and believe in your heart that Christ has been raised from the dead and you shall be saved." The misunderstanding is that the confession of Christ will bring about salvation. If this were true, then a deaf, mute person could not be saved because he would not be able to verbalize his belief on the Lord.

This is a fallacy that is also a travesty. Salvation is a free gift. If anyone can simply "make a decision" for Christ, then an act of grace is turned into a work and therefore, the believer can boast by saying "I made a decision!!!" No, Christ Himself is the One who has made the decision before the beginning of time as to those born on earth that He would call and grant "the free gift." At the appointed time, the one called to Christ is also chosen by Him to receive the faith to believe on the cross and the resurrection. Even the faith to believe on Him is not our own, but it is imparted to us by the Holy Ghost.

Preaching the gospel is the method by which the Holy Ghost plants the faith into the heart of the hearer. When the Holy Ghost plants faith into our hearts to believe on Jesus Christ, it may seem like we made the decision, when in all actuality, God Himself is the one who made the decision even prior to the fall of Adam, a call that we were compelled to heed and respond to His call. Consequently, the church cannot save anyone by having them repeat mere words. Nor does one get saved by "walking to the altar" as the Billy Graham Crusades imply.

The job of the church is simply to preach the gospel---Jesus crucified, dead, buried, raised and coming back to earth. That's the gospel in a nutshell. The church has truly failed "TO PREACH THE GOSPEL." Once the gospel is preached, then the rest of the work is between the hearer and the Holy Ghost. To try to browbeat people into salvation by preaching hell and damnation to force a decision for Christ is equally fruitless. The church has grieved and quenched the Holy Ghost by trying to do His job.

If you are one of those who came to Jesus solely by "making a decision," there is a good chance that you are not saved and the real real Jesus doesn't know you.

An Article by Pastor Pam : CHRISTIAN ZOMBIES

In 1988, Geraldo Rivera televised a program that centered on Christian Cults, with the subtitle "Zombies for Christ." Interviews were held with people who underwent deprogramming from the influence of charismatic, fundamentalist leaders and churches. The title seems apropos for this issue. In protecting the sheep, I suggest to you that we also need to examine the conditions of personality and circumstance that cause sheep to become "zombies for Christ." So the title of this article is: Christian Zombies.

In this hour, sheep are watching Christian television and reading Christian books, who themselves need to be deprogrammed from gross error that is causing them to be vulnerable to demonic oppression of a very serious nature. In fact, when I have tried to counsel those who have come to me to seek deliverance from the torment of demons, the mixture and error in their spiritual foundation is so deep, that deliverance is severely hindered by the amount of error that these captives have anchored their faith upon as they view

Christian television or read the books of various mega preachers. Almost 20 years have passed since the Rivera documentary. I suspect that the problem has intensified to the nth degree.

I am quite serious when I point out that I myself wonder if I must go through additional cleansing and purification due to Sananda's influence upon me. I had a dream this very week that clearly indicated that the occult leanings have lost all influence and strength in and upon me. At first, I rejoiced at this assurance. Then I remembered that the demons that are assigned to me read every word that I write. They hear my prayers and they know that I desire complete truth in my inward parts. So the message of this dream could very well have been inspired by the Sananda/Jezebel spirit to derail me and cause me a false assurance. I will continue to "watch, wait and pray."

In this regard, I had a true test this week in my email interactions with a reader that I will call "Maria." Maria's first email contact was relatively positive. (Check out her original commentary below). On the surface, it seemed that her intent was to merely apprise me that she and I have much in common in our backgrounds, and that she too believes that the prosperity gospel is coming down. I didn't notice at first but it seems she wanted me to publish her work on my website. I am a bit obtuse when people are not direct. However, I was truly amazed as well and somewhat concerned that Maria also wrote that she STILL feeds from the spiritual tables of Benny Hinn, Kenneth Copeland and Creflo Dollar, calling them "brothers that need prayer."

Not wanting to belittle Maria's prayer life, I really tried to be as "low key," as "laid back" as I myself can be, not expecting her extremely argumentative, defensive response. In her last email, Maria finally stated what she wanted to write in her first email, ie. that I am an "unloving accuser of the brethren." Yet, in keeping with the passivity of "a Christian Zombie," her hidden attitude was concealed until she could stand me no longer, and then all hell broke loose!!!! lol Finally, like a hissing snake she "cussed me out" Christian style. I was very brief and simple in my few responses so as not to stir up my own flesh, for actually, I was really not offended by her. So I tried to jest, keeping things light, remarking with "You would find a way to defend Judas Iscariot." She did not catch the humor, nor did she glean the meaning behind the humor. A common trait of those oppressed by a religious demon is that they tend to have no humor. Simply put, as Christian zombies they are so "spiritual" that they are of no earthly good.

Captives of this kind also rebel against any chastisement or correction with tongue in cheek counterattacks of "you're being "unloving" and therefore, you are not a real Christian. Yet zombies on the offensive usually pay no attention to the fact that the scriptures also declare that God Himself chastises and corrects those He loves. When He does chastise and correct, He often does so through elders and other saints. I personally believe that the epitomy of love is to tell someone liberating truth without belittling or shaming them. Truth that convicts rather than condemns. Of course, we are out to win the brethren and not to inflame them by provoking them to wrath. Certainly it is true that God so loved the world, yet He did not save Judas from perdition. As for me, I am in accord with Jesus Christ of Nazareth, who, when appropriate, didn't mind calling "a snake, a snake!" It is not wise to feed from the spiritual table of vipers.

Maria's emails continued to be abrupt, condescending and argumentative. Then there came a point when she realized that the tone of her emails was not "Christ-like", so she emailed me again, with a rather defensive apology. The " Christian zombie" thing for me to do was to passively accept her apology and stop the email war. True, but "I am not a Christian zombie!" It was clear to me that Maria's apology was based on her fear of facing her own persona---ie. that her "Christ like" image of herself was in jeopardy. To feed into her own self delusion would not be helpful. I have found that Christians who are constantly apologizing for being "who they are" "doing what they want to do" and saying "what they meant to say," generally are in bondage to obeying the word by the letter of the law rather than by the spirit. Since they are very "image conscious", they worry that they may be perceived as unloving or unmannerly and therein "not Christ-like". I view excessive demonstrations of this kind of anxiety as being a victim to the 3 false "p.s" THAT WHEN EXCESSIVE, CAUSES THEM TO BE a 4th "p" known as "PHONY": They are: PIETY, PRETENSE, AND PRIDE.

Walking in the "false p"s of self righteousness is yet another trademark of Christian zombies. I myself have encountered many professing Christians who speak "the love walk" with a forked tongue, whose hearts are deceived concerning what divine love actually is. The world can see through the hollowness of such people and sinners are not attracted to the Lord by a phony, self righteous witness. In my estimation, Maria is a classic example of a "Zombie for Christ." One reason is because Zombies always try to minimize deliverance and spiritual warfare ministries. In one of her emails, she accused me of being possessed by a demon that I have never heard of, identified as "the spirit of wrong focus." Maria explained that the "demon of wrong focus" causes watchmen like myself to be an "accuser of the brethren." She also stated that all she has to do is focus on the cross, pray for the "misguided" false prophets and trust God to deal with the devil for her. People who say "amen" to Maria are in danger of perishing for a lack of knowledge primarily because they underestimate the wiles of the enemy.

Another sign of a Christian zombie is their passive-aggressive hidden desire "to be heard." I can relate. I can remember that while I was in the denomination, for years I longed "to be heard" to no avail. I was often overlooked. Actually, a particular bishop purposefully and wilfully blocked my ministry, and rightly so. Even though he was operating out of his flesh in his strong dislike of me, I look pass this man's human nature and I perceive today "that it was the Lord's doing." For if I had not been blocked, then the seduction of a receptive audience would have been a major stumblingblock for me, deadly to my particular calling as a prophetic watchman. For as I stated in a previous issue, if I remained in the denomination,I was in bondage to too many levels of authority. The Lord warned me that I would never be more than a candle hidden under a defiled bed if I submitted myself to yet another denominational bishop or regional director.

Continually frustrated, disappointed and aggravated by denominational favoritism, I realize TODAY that I was truly blessed NOT to be have been embraced by the church hierarchy. The irony is that while I believed that my charismatic gifts to minister and my level of spiritual growth and understanding far surpassed that of the other denominational ministers, I myself was deceived. On the contrary, without the restraint of God, my charismatic leanings could have put countless sheep in an unprotected spiritual danger much more than ministries without power could have done. My spiritual error was just "different" from my denominational colleagues--- but error, none the less!! One of the greatest blessings that the Lord has ever given me for over two decades was "not to be heard." As the Apostle James warned, "Be not many masters because yours is the greater condemnation.

A review of Maria's emails clearly revealed that she is not yet ready to be heard. In retrospect, I deliberately refused to counterattack Maria's attempt to draw me into an email "scripture contest" just because I no longer pray for preachers to repent. This was a major part of my ministry for 25 years. I could be wrong but I believe that the season for those kinds of prayers is OVER! Also, contending "scripture for scripture" is not wise, nor is it scriptural. Any false prophet can contend with scripture, lifting up and upholding their own idolatrous practices with a scripture taken out of its context. It didn't take long for me to recognize the "works of Maria's flesh:" jealousy, ambition and envy."

Negative emotions of this kind oozed through every line of several emails that flooded my mail box--sometimes as many as 6 emails sent within minutes of each other. Then with her final email, her hidden agenda became self evident. The truth is that the spirit of Jezebel is really angry about this newsletter for "Maria" wrote and I quote: "Pam, you are living in a dream world and I fear you have a rude awakening coming if you think you are coming even close to representing Christ to the lost and the 'sheep' in your pen. There's no love there at all in your ministry, just the work of the accuser. Wake up before it's too late!!

Wow!!! It took a plethora of emails for Maria to finally allow the spirit of Jezebel to use her in a fullness. Since I realize that I do not contend with flesh and blood, I hold no ill will toward Maria. Therefore, if the Lord does cause her to sincerely repent, I will certainly receive her. Yet why did the Jezebelian demon choose Maria as its messenger? Well, because Maria is a very talented woman, an excellent writer who appears to be filled with zeal for Christ. Yet, she is ambitious, walking in the flesh of jealousy and a spirit of competition.

With all due respect, I must also commensurate with Maria's frustration. Those who have a call also have a strong desire to have a platform. Waiting on the Lord's timing can seem endless. However, as we wait, the Lord requires a very deep allegiance to the truth. He invariably will set up circumstances that will cause us to bow down to correction which cuts and humbles, as readily as we accept that which is agreeable. The Lord has cut me down so often in 30 years, that I myself am not used to being well received. So quite the opposite, I have been humbled by those who have so graciously embraced my articles with such eagerness, affection and appreciation. Some of you have written and even spoken to me personally, expressing how much each one of them has meant to you and for that, I rejoice.

Nevertheless, it is very important for us all to realize that other than for witchcraft, works of the flesh are not "cast out." Even those demons that specialize in witchcraft have different names. So for the most part, works of the flesh are "put off" or "pulled down" but not "cast out." The truth is that an ambitious, jealous person needs his or her flesh crucified through the brokenness of repentance and the fires of refinement. This is the work of "deliverance counseling." As a therapist, one of my strategies is to cause both the saved and the unsaved to examine and understand the nature of their particular "flesh style". Why? Well, because demons take advantage of the flesh to mobilize their own agenda. Consequently, knowing ourselves better than the demons know us is a primary step to "trying the spirits." We must try our own spirits to understand the nature of our own particular needs of the flesh. The truth received will crush that need or in other words, "crucify our flesh.!"

One of the greatest revelations that I have discovered out of years of the 5 "T"S of testing, temptation, trial, tribulation and trouble is that "we are never as advanced as we believe ourselves to be." Merely having spiritual experiences does not make us "spiritual." What makes us "spiritual" is abiding in Christ. To abide means to live, move and have our being in Him, consistently and steadfastly. In other words, to abide is " STANDING STRONG, PRESSING FORWARD AND NOT LOOKING BACK UNTIL YOU HAVE BEEN YOKED TO JESUS AS A VINE IS TO A BRANCH!!!"I admit that in the first two decades, I had more spiritual experiences than I can now count or even remember.

Nevertheless, one has become really "spiritual" when one can face the truth without flinching. Moreover, what I have learned is that when truth explodes upon the mind, it is not an agreeable experience, nor is it easy to disbelieve absolutely, what we have consistently believed so thoroughly. Once I committed myself to truth, I find that I no longer depend on signs or supernatural experiences. The knowledge and wisdom received in the last 3 years, and even more so, the last 3 months have been astounding.
I

So, if you have been a zombie for Christ in your church,when your eyes have finally been opened, look out!!! Being deceived can be taken as a personal insult. To perceive that we have been duped:

bamboozled, run a muck, gone astray, hoodwinked, made a fool of. Don't even go there in your thoughts about all of that hard earned money we put into the hands of religious demons. Lord, Help!!!!

Surprisingly, religious zombies are often created out of their own zeal to please God with their flesh. As a Pharisee, Saul of Tarsus was a good example prior to his Damascus Road experience, persecuting and killing Christians, even consenting to the stoning to death of Stephen. The essential pattern is that Christian zombies want to die so that Christ can live in them, therefore fulfilling Paul's words of "I am crucified with Christ, nevertheless I live, not I, but Christ who lives in me." They concentrate very heavily on the "not I." Even when referring to themselves in writing, some of them use "i" in the small case to signify to all who commune with them that Christ has rulership in their lives and in everything they say and do, it is "Christ doing the speaking and the doing" and not them. On the contrary, the Holy Ghost is a Helper. He does not take over the human vessel like a puppet master. He helps us do the work by using all of our human faculties, including our personalities.

    In short, the nature of zombies for Christ is that the spiritual concept of dying in and for Him has been misinterpreted and grossly misunderstood. Some have gotten confused through wrong preaching or by reading a book on the subject that they were not spiritually mature enough to understand. For example, some have read Watchman Nee's several books on the flesh, but they really did not understand that Nee was not an advocate of killing the human personality. Simply put, the zombies seek to be dead while they are alive, with deadness manifesting as passivity, including the tacit accepting of suffering and a relishing in weakness. In other words, for Christ to live in them, they must be frail and insignificant---taking their own crucifixion to the extreme of passivity and a restraint of personality by submitting their entire life space to the conviction that "everything happens to them by the order of God."

    Mis-interpreting the scripture concerning Paul's "thorn in the side" and his statements to the Galatians and the Corinthians about being crucified with Christ, Christian zombies relish in human weakness, not realizing that Paul was not suggesting that "he chose to be weak." On the contrary, Paul never denied the need for human strength. No, he simply learned that at those unplanned times when weakness DID come upon him, the Lord's grace was there to rescue him.

Consequently, as a zombie for Christ begins to relish in weakness as a condition of being filled with the Holy Ghost, evil spirits revel in seducing and deceiving them. In fact, it is actually demons who have orchestrated the circumstances in the first place, so as to create snares by which to entrap them, taking advantage of a faithful believer's desire to please and serve God. This is why false prophets have been successful at duping the sheep. With a lack of knowledge, he sheep have prepared themselves for the slaughter of wolves, to be victimized by a misguided understanding of what it really takes to please God.

Although the Christian Zombie's path may seem commendable, if we are not careful, the enemy will use our faithfulness to the cross according to our misunderstanding of what Paul actually means concerning being crucified with Christ. The danger is that our misunderstanding will cause us to wrongfully accept all suffering and therein become a zombie--- battered about by the world, our loved ones, the flesh and the devil. We must do all that we can to stand, and having done all to stand, WE STAND!

As we stand, we must give no place to the devil by our passivity. We MUST aggressively resist him at every turn. For example, choosing weakness and choosing suffering both fulfill the requirements for the operation of demons since by so doing, our free will is placed on the enemy's side. God wants us to cooperate with Him but He does NOT desire to control us like puppets or like zombies. Nor does He desire to destroy our personalities. Neither does He demand our minds. We need to understand that anger is an important human emotion, God given in fact. Yet, as the word of God warns, we can BE ANGRY but we must not allow our anger to cause us to sin. Jesus Christ of Nazareth knows that our thoughts are not His thoughts and our ways are not His ways, yet He does not command us to change ourselves. I repeat that in John 15, lasting change comes from "abiding in Him." Once we are no longer conformed or habituated to this world system, we are transformed by the renewing of our minds. (Romans 12:1,2) Over time, we begin to think as He thinks, and progressively and eventually our own thoughts die without any real effort of our own.

Renewal comes from delighting in Jesus Christ of Nazareth yet you need to know that Sananda can manufacture a false sense of peace and refreshing.. (Psalm 37:4) As we continue to delight in the true Lord, without our even noticing, He gives us the desires of our hearts. In other words, the more we get to know Him, the more of Christ gets planted in our hearts, a result of the cooperation of our own free wills. As we are "crucified daily," the Lord's desires become planted in our hearts very imperceptibly and low and behold, His desires are now our desire. In fact, we don't even know or recognize the moment that the transformation occurred when we were able to declare, "it is not I who live but Christ who lives in me." It just "happens." As the wind blows where it wills, one day we simply notice that we have begun to think and to act differently---more like Christ. Yet like the buds appear on a tree in spring time, we never able to see our transformation coming, nor can we describe it with any accuracy.

Satan is just the opposite. To make his work easier, demons demand that his zombies become passive in their will. Counterfeiting God,demons deceive zombies to deny the use of either part or all of their human abilities. Clearly, the fake Jesus is the unseen creator of the Christian zombie. If undetected, the Jezebel spirit will proceed to destroy a Christian's personality. Jezebel will take pleasure in reducing him (usually her) to a zombie state, subdue his or her soul and body. Finally, the zombie is left unprotected, ravaged by the spiritual abuse of wolves in sheeps' clothing, spiritually oppressed and imprisoned by demonic soul ties to the oppressors. This religious demon puts the unsuspecting Christian under the oppression of a force that appears to represent God's will and compels the Christian zombie to act like a machine, devoid of reason, thought or decision.

To cap things off with a quote from "Faces of the Religious Demon", there is hope through taking personal responsibility and never allowing ourselves to accept the role of "victim.":

> It is my belief that captives will become free of the mental and emotional damage incurred by the spiritual abuse afflicted upon them by others when they can accept full responsibility for allowing themselves to be spiritually victimized. A captive who has faced himself can only see or feel in the flesh because he has been blinded from true self perception in the spirit. Therefore, he may find it difficult to recognize how much of his own sensitivities, his hidden hostilities, as well as his own exacting demands for attention may have interfered with his relationships and actually drew him to controlling people. Without facing his true self, when he actually does find a genuinely assertive leader, the captive may unconsciously set up situations to try to compel the new leader to attempt to control his life." (Faces, pg. 228)

Works of the flesh such as jealousy and ambition (Galatians 5) are debilitating character defects that cause frustrated ministers and "wannabees" to have "a strong lust to be heard." As previously indicated, since jealousy and ambition are not demons as some deliverance ministers believe, it is useless to try to cast them out. The reason why the casting out of demons is not always successful, is primarily because the ground that gave the demons their occupation cannot be cast out. This is why counseling is crucial to deal with flesh issues. For example, jealousy and ambition are components of the ground of human flesh that will give the Jezebel spirit its doorway. Unless the ground of the human soul is dealt with, no full relief from demons can be obtained in the majority of cases where the flesh has not been crucified through repentance and brokenness. Often we are duped to believe that demons have been cast out because of the power of the human will. However, human will power DOES HAVE the capacity to suppress behavior and cause a captive to appear to be delivered. However, since the ground has not effectively been dealt with, the same manifestation can return and repeat itself in a different disguise ie. like a former alcoholic becoming an addicted gambler.

I define the flesh as character traits of human nature without Christ, defects that cannot be CAST OUT. (Galatians 5:) Human nature can never please God. I could be wrong, but I do not believe that demons will respond by calling them "the spirit of jealousy" or "the spirit of ambition." No, the demon who has those traits is the religious demon, aka, the Jezebel spirit, the Judas spirit or the spirit of the anti-Christ. Demons of this kind are attracted to people who manifest narcissism in the form of self love, conceit, jealousy and ambition. Jessie Penn Lewis in "War on the Saints" provides a salient warning to those who would minimize or underestimate the need to be vigilant and prepared for both deliverance and spiritual warfare. Her words remind me of the scripture,"be not many masters because yours is the greater condemnation:

"If we liken the war by prayer, systematically carried out against the forces of darkness, to a war in the natural sphere, those who would lead must be willing to to be trained, and to take the same learner's attitude as a recruit in the natural sphere. Such believers need to obtain knowledge of the organized hosts of darkness, and how to exercise their spiritual vision so that 'by reason of use', it becomes acute in discerning the operations of the enemy in the spiritual sphere. The believer must learn to observe, and learn by observation their methods in the war against the people of God." (War on the Saints, pg.

265-266)

As I continue to practice deliverance counseling, I have observed that once clients have been armed with self knowledge, with an awareness of who they are in Christ and they accept the fact that they themselves have played a major role in their own captivity, virtually all demons will leave on their own accord without even a need to perform a deliverance. However, there are two demons that will put up a formidable fight: the Jezebel Spirit and the spirit of the anti-Christ. Because of these two demons, the deliverance counseling model was designed.

Therefore, Christian Zombies will have to humble themselves to the fact that their spiritual experience may be filled with deception. For to really be crucified with Christ does not mean that the life of your personality has to be annihilated. To bare our cross is to learn how to endure hardship as good soldiers. To bare our cross is to surrender our desire for acceptance as we become increasingly separated from the seductions of the world. Notwithstanding, the real and present danger is that the organized church has become "the church world," filled with seductions that appeal to the flesh NOT being crucified. In truth, much of what we need to be crucified from emanates from our connection to the organized church.

In this regard, I am reminded of a dream I had just last night about a former ministerial colleague whom I upheld as my best friend for 20 years. In the dream, he revealed the true nature of his heart and declared, "I did not come to your aid, nor did I support you even with a phone call, because I couldn't risk incurring the bishop's wrath upon myself for being in fellowship with you. I wanted the bishop to appoint me to the church that I now pastor. Even though I knew what was being done to you was unfair, I had to look out for myself." This is the nature of much of the organized church: filled with competition, striving, self-interest and jealousy, one minister striving to outshine another.

Unless pride is broken in ALL of us, the religious demon will remain in control and our service for Christ will be at risk for and subject to contamination. Nevertheless, as Christian zombies gain victories over the deception of the enemy by recognizing, resisting, and triumphing over them in our varied workings, our strength of spirit to conquer demons will grow stronger and stronger. In fact, we will be transformed from wimps to warriors. Actually, we will discover that even though we have been crucified with Christ, WE STILL LIVE, not by our own power but by the power of the Holy Ghost. This is truly being Christlike--- Zombies, NO MORE!!!

WHAT'S MISSING?

YOU GO TO CHURCH REGULARLY, YET.....

Are you struggling with serious bondages like fear, depression, voices in your mind, strange dreams, mental illness, physical illness, torments of all kinds?

Are you still in bondage to the addictions, not only drugs and alcohol but sex and other addictions?

Do you feel uncomfortable speaking to church leadership about your particular bondage for various reasons, one of which is that your church does not deal with problems of its kind?

Has the assurance of your salvation escaped you and therefore you have not reaped any spiritual fruit from "going to church?" In other words, has "going to church" in itself become just another habit, bordering on an addiction?

You believe that it is only by the blood of Jesus that your sins are forgiven, yet do you really FEEL forgiven or does sin STILL HAVE dominion over you?

Are you hiding a secret sin from your local church, not only deceiving them but also deceiving yourself?

So do you "fake it" to "make it?"

Do you belong to a word of faith or charismatic church where the gifts of the Holy Spirit are preached and taught about often, yet the manifestations you have witnessed are "questionable?"

Do you belong to a dry, dying, and/or defiled denominational church, where sin is tolerated and the preaching is weak and ineffectual? Are you hooked to "a form of godliness that denies the power by your traditions that make the word of God of none effect?"

Have you been tithing and/or giving offerings, yet God has not provided you with the material blessings that church leadership continue to teach you are "yours for the asking" yet God has not answered?

Do you obtain all of your spiritual nourishment from Christian television? Are you hero-worshiping a mega preacher?

Are you suspecting that your bondage is connected to invisible entities called "demons?"

If you have answered "yes" to even one of these questions, than there is much reading material on this website that can provide you with the answers you seek. We recommend that besides the free articles on this website, that you also consider purchasing the books below. However, if you need personal, "hands on" help to guide you towards recovery and restoration, then click here. You can also call 518-477-7385 to make an appointment for telephone counseling, mentoring or enroll in training.

Then there are others.

You are not a churchgoer, but you are a seeker of "spirituality." As such, have you ever been involved with false religions? Examples of false religions are Buddhism, Hindu, eastern religions, and false Christian religions like Jehovah Witness, Mormonism, Catholicism, Oneness Pentecostals, Freemasonry, Christian Science and several others.

Have you dabbled with the occult, ie. astrology, frequenting psychics, mediums and fortune tellers, partaken of astral travel, communication with the dead (necromancy), Santeria, WICCA, transcendental meditation, yoga, crystals, pyramids, biofeedback, automatic writing, hypnosis, reincarnation and other forms and practices of witchcraft and idolatry?

If you can answer in the affirmative to either of these questions, this website is for you also. You can find help by contacting us at deliverancecounseling.com

What is truly important to your spiritual wellbeing is how you answer the following questions:

Do you desire truth and freedom?
 Are you willing to do what must be done to be set free?

Are you willing to pick up the cross and follow Jesus by your surrender and obedience to Him as Lord?
Are you willing to give up the things that provided doorways to demonic activity?
Are you prepared to make any necessary lifestyle changes in order to keep obtain qnd to keep your deliverance? If your answer to all five of these questions is "yes", then this website is for you also. For additional information, send an email to <u>beware911@yahoo.com</u> <u>or call toll free: 877-726-7911.</u>

THERE ARE STILL OTHERS!!!

You are a mature follower of Jesus Christ. Some of you are active church members but you are "frustrated" with the lack of spiritual growth of those around you, and so you are really a loner. Most church folk do not understand you so they either tolerate you because "you are there," or they avoid you because they consider you to be "strange." Some of you are not churchgoers, yet the Lord is guiding you anyway. If you are looking for strong yet non-judgemental guidance and direction, our mentoring program is for you.

Once you spend some time on our websites at bewarechristian.com or deliverancecounseling.com, you may decide that you would like to be either pastored, mentored or perhaps you are interested in hands on training by telephone and unlimited emails that will answer your personal questions. We welcome you and your uniqueness. Send us an email to <u>beware911@yahoo.com</u> if "this is YOU!"

ALPHABETICAL INDEX

America, 34, 79, 163
Angels.........27, 116, 162, 176
ANTI-CHRIST..15, 22, 44, 50, 52-55,, 61,80,84, 87,103, 130, 182, 196 ,211
ASCENDED MASTER 7,10, 15, 22, 28, 36, 38, 44, 54, 58-60, 67-79, 100, 105, 112. 115-118
ASHTAR 28-36
   baptism...136, 142, 148
Azusa Street 136, 147
BAILEY, Alice 61, 90, 100, 105, 176
bewarechristian.com, 181, 217
BLAVATSKY,Helen 61,86,102,107,180
Brown, Rebecca, 152
   BYNUM, Juanita 140

captives.. 8, 37, 120, 154, 200, 210
CATHOLICISM   110
   Roman Catholics,18, 46, 63, 66, 95, 108, 154, 187, 215
   Catholic Apostolic 144
Chakras   97
   channel.....32, 40,45, 56, 77, 80, 82, 114
CHARISMATIC, 7, 17, 26, 47, 58, 109, 115, 125, 128, 144, 147, 150-154, 172-174, 199, 203, 214
   charismania...136
CHRISTIANITY, 64, 96, 150, 179, 182
   Christians, general, 11, 17, 25, 46, 51,61, 74,84, 94, 96, 102, 109, 111, 124, 134, 150, 154, 163, 169, 171,
      Christian Zombies, 199, 212
         Christian Yoga, 94
CHURCH, 170, 181, 190, 214
   at Philadelphia 136
   at Laodicea 67,135, 141
   at Thyatira, 108, 110m 112m 117
 church, 5, 7, 9, 16, 18, 25, 42, 45, 49, 56, 60, 64, 72, 80, 83, 92, 95, 99, 101, 103, 105, 112, 115, 117, 120, 124, 134, 138, 141, 149, 154, 181, 202, 206, 212
   condemnation, 89, 204, 211
   confusion, 18, 51, 111, 127, 136

consciousness altering, 54, 67
counseling, 38, 50, 107,118, 124, 131, 154, 167, 181, 185,193, 105, 211, 215
crucified, 125, 127, 139, 191, 198, 205, 207, 211
    crucifixion.c..125, 128, 207
Counterfeit---12, 17, 27, 30, 46, 58, 69, 93, 98, 100, 102, 105, 118, 134, 151, 153, 186, 194
cults 9, 16, 21, 29, 105, 114, 120, 171,199
    CREME, Benjamin, 56

DECEPTION, 12, 20, 25, 45, 52, 55, 79, 89, 91, 93, 98, 100, 112, 121, 134, 138, 212
deliverance counseling, 2, 107, 181, 216
DELIVERANCE..7,38, 107, 128, Christian Zombies, 199, 212
    Christian Yoga, 96
DEMONS, demonic 9, 11, 16, 21, 24, 27, 35, 38, 43, 45, 52, 61, 69, 75, 79, 80,90, 96, 99, 102, 107, 112, 117, 124,133, 139,152,156,167,171,182,188,193,195,200,205,208
DENOMINATION, 58, 66,96, 109, 122, 125, 130, 139, 144, 150, 1254, 170, 184, 192, 203, 214
detachment...................95-99
dominion theology, 18, 79, 81
dreams, 8, 589, 68,73, 189, 214

earth, 29,37, 44, 77, 114, 116, 134, 146, 157, 163, 182, 192,201
endtimes, 11, 18, 54, 68, 100, 133
error, 51, 114, 121, 138, 155, 163, 190, 199,203
    Elijah, 33, 133
    ETTER, Marie-Woodworth 146, 178
EVANGELISTS-(TV,)15, 20, 28, 103, 122, 122, 137, 139, 147, 150, 163, 172, 186,

FAITH, 7, 17, 22, 28, 33, 42, 45, 47, 49, 58, 64, 84, 87, 103, 109, 116, 125, 137, 2140, 142, 147, 152, 154, 1261, 166, 171, 187, 191, 196, 198, 200, 208, 214
FAKE JESUS, 5, 7,9, 13, 16, 25, 28,
FALSEFIRE 132-13638,43,46,67,69,107,116,124,130,134,157,171
FINNEY, Charles 122,129, 130,138,178
  flesh, 12, 27, 54,68, 72, 82, 84, 89, 100,106, 127,

129,139, 149,164, 185, 201, 203, 210
    fornication, 8 108, 110, 141, 168
    freedom 6,33, 81,163, 177,216
    freemasonry, 21, 76, 80, 138, 147
        fruit 167
fear, 37,50,71,87,102,126,188,202, 204,214

GOD'S PEOPLE, 9,18, 23,65, 95,99,142, 163
GOSPEL, 18, 47, 73, 109, 121, 125,127,130, 132, 136-142, 155, 170, 189, 191.197.200
GOLDEN AGE, 44,176

  HEALING, DIVINE 136-138
      history, 7, **58**, 63, 65,73, 76, 79, 91, 102, 132, 134, 142, 143, 154, 156, 168, 178, 188
    holiness 143, 150
        holy laughter, 139
        holy dancing, 139
        spontaneous 140

idolatry, 8, 110, 146, 155, 187, 215
IRVING, Edward, 136, 144
    impostor, 13, 25, 40, 43, 118, 169, 209
      ISRAEL, 63

JESUS CHRIST OF NAZARETH
6,9,12, 16, 18, 27, 36, 44, 46, 52, 55, 60, 69, 91, 93, 97, 99, 103, 107, 117, 121, 124, 128, 146, 161, 165, 201, 209
JEZEBEL 61-64
JUDGMENT.......9,17,99,122,149,157,179
KING, George 44,176
    Oprah, 29, 33, 35
KUHLMAN, Kathryn 137,140, 180

Levites....63

MAITREYA,15,23,43,56-60, 81,85,91,93,100,105,118,120,164,170,176,195
Make a Decision Gospel, ,122, 138
  martyrs.....84

masochism....120
masonic...77,81
masquerade, 13, 24, 54, 68, 76
MEGA 20, 47, 51,79, 132, 136, 140, 147, 162, 168, 185, 191, 194,200, 215
mentoring, 50, 215
MINISTRY 15, 40, 50, 63, 65, 82, 102, 110, 135, 138, 151, 159, 167, 171, 178, 182, 184, 186, 192, 194, 203
misinterpret 191,198, 207
MISSION 2, 35, 38,45, 60,107, 116, 121, 137, 140, 148, 189
176,195
Mormons, 35, 46,106, 137, 145, 171
MOTHER ANN LEE 143
MOTHER MARY 15, 24, 53, 107-111, **114-118**, 120,
Mother Ship 30,34,163
MYSTERY BABYLON,67, 100, 130, 163, 174

Nation of Islam, 25,33-34
necromancy, 10, 138, 215
NEW AGE, 9, 10, 24, 38, 43, 53-54, 59, 67, 70, 102, 105, 112, 114-116, 118, 176
Noah, 12, 28, 54, 68, 72
occultism, 53, 114, 120, 138
Oprah, 29, 33, 35
ouija board 57, 71, 88

PARHAM, Charles 146
passivity, 61, 72, 95, 97-98, 101, 201, 207
pastor 19, 144, 162, 166, 170, 181, 183, 190, 192, 213, 217
PASTOR PAM, 7, 15, 20, 22, 38, 55, 71, 73, 80, 87, 101, 131, 147, 156, 163, 166, 174, 199
PENTECOSTAL 17, 42, 47, 109, 122, 137M 141, 144, 147, 149, 150,154, 174, 186-187, 215
prophesy 37, 145

PROTESTANTISM 66, 109 121-156,
    Presbyterian, 105,144

rapture   30, 83, 123,138,189
    Red Sea   167
reincarnation 24,73, 112, 116, 215
RELIGIOUS 9, 16, 18, 20, 22, 29,33, 37, 43, 45, 47, 55, 61, 69, 84, 89, 110, 123, 130, 133, 144, 147, 152, 164, 170, 183, 186, 189, 194, 201, 206, 210, 213
REPENT   9,20, 67, 70, 90, 108, 112, 116, 123, 128, 134, 148, 169, 181, 188, 192, 197, 204, 211
RESURRECTION 6, 19,46, 53, 56, 63, 106, 126, 169, 188, 195
    resuscitated   70
        righteousness 93, 173, 192, 202
ROBERTS, Oral   137, 180

SAINT GERMAIN 15,53,**75-83**
        Salvation, (see saved)
SANANDA, 15, 25, 28, 37, **44-55** 53, 81, 112, 116, 118, 120, 130, 164, 169, 175, 195, 200, 209
      SATAN, 6, 10, 17, 22, 25, 27, 36, 43, 45, 52, 60, 67, 70, 80, 83, 89, 112, 121, 130, 133, 140, 146, 151, 153, 157, 182, 188, 194, 209 202,208,216
SAVED, 6, 10, 12, 18, 47, 55, 73, 89, 114, 117, **121-124**, 128, 131, 143, 146, 155, 168, 171, 173, 183, 187, 190, 193, 196
SAVIOR 72, 97, 102, 106, 111,
   seduction   87, 89, 139, 203, 212
      sex, sexuality,   9, 12, 28, 81, 105, 109, 118, 146, 150, 173, 214
SEYMORE, William 147, 179
      sickness and disease, 42, 101, 137, 140
   Shakers 143
 SIGNS   ..11, 27, 72, 112, 121, 130, 132, 140, 159, 163,206
                  SIN 197, 206, 214
SMITH, Joseph, 137, **144-145**, 179
      sickness 148, 179
SPIRIT.. 3, 5, 7, 10, 15, 20, 24, 27, 37, 46, 51, 54, 57,63, 67, 70, 76, 82, 85, 94, 98, 100, 103, 105, 110, 112., 114, 118, 123, 126, 130, 132, 134, 139, 143, 146,

149, 158, 164, 170, 174, 181, 184, 188, 193, 195, 200,
   HOLY SPIRIT 2, 8, 40, 44, 60, 71, 82, 117, 121, 143, 146, 153, 155, 166, 171, 187, 190, 212, 214
     spirit guide   71, 88
THE FATHER, 11, 27, 18, 65, 70, 76, 96, 99, 103, 106, 118, 123, 126, 146, 155, 160, 166
THE TRUE JESUS   18, 44, 46, 116, 129, 157, 187
The Great White Brotherhood, 23, 175
The Wales Revival   150
Thedra, Sister   40, 42, 175
   Thessalonian, 56, 157
     tithing 197, 214
 Tongues, speaking in other 17, 68, 95, 100, 136, 142, 151, 169, 187, 196
TORMENT 8, 37, 61, 69, 96, 107, 154, 169, 200, 214
TREE   .5, 8, 73, 131, 135, 141, 144, 149, 166, 172, 185, 209
     tribulation, 67, 79, 84, 93, 134, 165, 206
    TRIMM, Cindy 15
   TRUDEL, Dorethea, 137

undeceive 134, 142
UNIFICATION CHURCH 107

violence 90, 115
   voices, 61, 88, 214

WALK-IN 70, **71**, 176
WAR ON THE SAINTS 97, 151, 188, 211
   wonders, 112, 133
World Trade Center 92, 162
WORD OF FAITH 7, 112, 133, 142, 174

YOGA   44, 54, 61, 67, 96, 177, 215

www.ingramcontent.com/pod-product-compliance
Lightning Source LLC
Chambersburg PA
CBHW020756160426
43192CB00006B/347